Controlling Unlawful
Organizational Behavior

D0777581

Controlling Unlawful Organizational Behavior

Social Structure and Corporate Misconduct

Diane Vaughan

The University of Chicago Press *Chicago and London*

THE UNIVERSITY OF CHICAGO PRESS, CHICAGO 60637
THE UNIVERSITY OF CHICAGO PRESS, LTD., LONDON

©1983 by The University of Chicago
All rights reserved. Published 1983
Paperback edition 1985
Printed in the United States of America
94 93 92 91 90 89 88 87 86 85   2 3 4 5 6

LIBRARY OF CONGRESS CATALOGING IN PUBLICATION DATA

Vaughan, Diane.
    Controlling unlawful organizational behavior.

    (Studies in crime and justice)
    Bibliography: p.
    Includes index.
    1. White collar crimes—United States.   2. Corporations
—United States—Corrupt practices.   3. Interorganiza-
tional relations—United States.   4. Computer crimes—
United States.   5. Organizational behavior—Case studies.
6. Revco Drug Stores, Inc.—Case studies.   I. Title.
II. Series.
HV6768.V38   1983   364.1′06′073   83–3489
ISBN 0-226-85171-0 (cloth)
ISBN 0-226-85174-5 (paper)

To my parents and my children

Contents

Acknowledgments

This book grew out of two intellectual environments: Ohio State University, where I did my graduate work, and Yale University, where I continued the project as an NIMH postdoctoral fellow. The research began at Ohio State as my doctoral dissertation. The study was made possible by the willingness of many officials to discuss their work with me. Although the promise of confidentiality prevents me from mentioning individual names, I gratefully acknowledge the help of the members of the Ohio Department of Public Welfare, the Ohio State Board of Pharmacy, the Economic Crime Unit of the Franklin County Prosecutor's Office, and the Ohio State Highway Patrol, without whose cooperation this research would not have been possible. I was guided by an exceptional dissertation committee: Simon Dinitz, chair, Richard J. Lundman, and John Seidler. Their diverse perspectives, insights, criticisms, encouragement, and humor were invaluable to my development as a sociologist and to this work. Lynn A. Oberg, Certified Financial Analyst, also added significantly to the research. More informal but important contributions were made by John P. Conrad, Ronald G. Corwin, and Judith A. DiIorio.

At Yale, my fellowship gave me, for the first time, a room of my own and the luxury of time to think and to write. As a consequence, I had the opportunity to develop fully the theoretical framework of the book which I had briefly outlined in the last chapter of my dissertation. This development was enhanced by my participation in two seminars which provided me with the collegial exchange so essential to the development of ideas. Albert J. Reiss, Jr., and the members of the postdoctoral seminar "The Sociology of Social Control" critiqued multiple drafts of each chapter with patience and insight. My thanks, also, to Kai T.

Erikson and the writing seminar members for enriching not only the style, but the substance of this book.

Patricia M. Ewick's comments on early drafts have added significantly to the precision and logic of my ideas. Others to whom I am indebted are Scott A. Boorman, Mimi Bean, Marlene Brask, Edward M. Cane, Burton R. Clark, William M. Evan, Gilbert Geis, Edward Gross, Gary T. Marx, Walter W. Powell, Neal Shover, Richard I. Werder, Jr., Stanton Wheeler, and William F. Whyte. My research was supported in part by Grant No. 2T32 MH15123 from the National Institute of Mental Health. For encouragement, counsel, and understanding that were essential to the research, to the book, and to myself, I thank Peter M. Gerhart. For my parents, my aunt, and my children—Roger, Lisa, and Susan—no words of thanks will ever be enough.

Introduction

Picture a room filled with grey metal desks. At each desk sits a welfare department social worker interviewing clients. An elderly woman with a shopping bag sits with others on a bench along the wall waiting her turn. At a nod from her social worker, she goes to the wooden chair beside the desk, rummages through her purse for some papers, then empties the contents of the shopping bag on the desk. Prescription medication bottles spill out. For the next forty minutes the welfare recipient and the social worker sort through the bottles, comparing the prescription numbers on each bottle with a list of prescription numbers on a letter sent to the woman by the welfare department. The purpose of the letter is to verify that she did, in fact, receive the goods the pharmacy records indicate she received.

This scene typifies the sweeping changes in health care delivery in this country. For large segments of the population—the blind, the poor, the aged, and the dependent—obtaining goods and services related to health is no longer an exchange between the seeker and provider of services; the encounter has now expanded to include the government, which formulates the rules for the exchange. Nursing homes, pharmacies, hospitals, dentists, physicians, and ambulance services sign contracts with federal, state, or local government program sponsoring agencies to deliver their specialized goods and services to the public. These providers are then reimbursed in accordance with established guidelines and regulations.

The entire system is built upon a network of increasingly specific and intricate rules—rules which affect whole classes of individuals and organizations. Providers as well as recipients must meet eligibility requirements to participate, the government must distinguish between those goods and services for which reimbursement will and those for which it will not be allowed, providers must adopt procedures for seeking reimbursement that conform to federal guidelines, federal agencies require reports of state and local programs, which in turn require filing by providers, caseworkers, recipients—and on and on. The rules are directed at standardization and control. Yet not only has standardization not been achieved, but attempts to impose order have spawned disorder. Benefit programs are accused of excessive red tape, burdensome paperwork, inadequate verification of data, and poor quality control.[1] Significantly, these administrative weaknesses have created what insiders call "program vulnerability": they present multiple opportunities within the benefit programs for individuals, groups, or organizations to take unintended or illegal advantage of the system.[2]

And take advantage they have. Fraud and abuse of government benefit programs are widespread.[3] To combat the losses, federal, state, and local governments have committed substantial audit, investigation, and computer resources to detection. On 28 July 1977, for example, Revco Drug Stores, Inc., one of the nation's largest retail drug chains and a Medicaid provider, was found guilty of a computer-generated double-billing scheme that resulted in the loss of over a half million dollars in Medicaid funds to the Ohio Department of Public Welfare. The case is unique, yet indicative of a serious and changing trend in the nature of unlawful behavior in our society. Where once both offender and victim were individuals, in this instance both roles were played by complex organizations, and the definition of who was offender and who was victim was not so clear. Further, the intricacies of the Revco case were deepened by the use of computer technology, both in the commission and the investigation of the unlawful conduct. The complexities were such that were it not for a serendipitous series of events, the offense would not have been discovered at all. Moreover, the impenetrability of both the offense and the offender necessitated the involvement of not just one but five investigative agencies in the discovery, investigation, and prosecution of this case. In the absence of any single formal mechanism to deal with this type of misconduct, these five organizations pooled their specialized skills and resources, forming a social control network to pursue the wayward corporation.

The details of the Revco case and investigation tantalize the sociologist, for this event indicates significant social change: change in the nature of crime—and in the way society organizes to combat it. Unlawful behavior by organizations is a natural consequence of the transformation of social structure. Not only do individuals interact with individuals; now they interact with organizations, and organizations interact with other organizations.[4] These new sets of relationships have affected opportunities for unlawful behavior. The roles of victim and offender are no longer restricted to individuals. Organizations can and do assume either role, and frequently—as in the Revco case—both. The parallel development is the emergence and growth of regulatory agencies, such as the FTC and SEC, directed toward controlling organizational misconduct. This occurrence has been so widespread that the monitoring and regulation of corporate interactions has itself become "big business," with the complexity of the regulatory agency at times matching or even exceeding that of the organizations it regulates. The Revco investigation stimulated my curiousity about these developments. The result is this book, which addresses two major questions: (1) how, in this case, did society organize to combat the unlawful behavior of an organization, and (2) in what ways is society organized that may encourage the very phenomenon it purports to restrain?

The pages that follow are shaped by three strongly held personal beliefs. First, the behavior of organizations should be understood within the context of the social structure in which it occurs. Thus, I examine the Revco case within the immediate social structure, delineated for research purposes by the interaction of the organizations that participated in the event, and then I examine the broader structure of American society for factors relevant to the origin and control of organizational misconduct. Second, given the rise of regulatory agencies to control corporate conduct over the last several decades, merging conceptual tools and knowledge of interorganizational relations with what is known about organizational misconduct is a logical and fruitful step. To date, however, there has been a clear, if unarticulated, division of labor among sociologists. The interaction of organizations has been primarily the realm of those with expertise in complex organizations; the unlawful behavior of organizations has been the subject of research by those interested in deviance and social control.

This book is couched in a framework that merges these two sub-disciplines of sociology.

Third, field research that reveals the little-understood intricacies of these interorganizational relationships is the most appropriate research style. Consequently, the data were gathered in what amounted to five case studies, one conducted in each of the social control agencies that investigated the case. The information was obtained through interviews with members of the agencies, lawyers, legislators, financial analysts, stockbrokers, and reporters. These interview data were supplemented by materials in agency files, government reports, newspaper articles, interorganizational memos, and official documents related to the case.

My original hope for this research was that I could develop an analysis of the case that included both sides of the story. Not that there existed some objective truth that could be uncovered by blending or comparison, but that for Revco and for those doing the investigating there were separate realities: a truth for each side. The best I could do was to portray as holistic a representation of what happened as possible by presenting each of these realities. Unfortunately, because Revco did not participate in the research, this book is based on only one. Yet how the network organizations went about their work is relevant, documented, and worthy of inquiry and attention. This is so, regardless of that "other side of the story" that has remained elusive.

The History
of the Case

May 1976

An alert pharmacist in an Ohio Revco Drug Store noticed that a neighborhood podiatrist had been prescribing large quantities of narcotics and tranquilizers—medications that appeared to be outside the scope of podiatry practice. Alarmed, the pharmacist called the Ohio State Board of Pharmacy. The pharmacy board quietly initiated an investigation.[1]

July 1976

A vice-president from Revco headquarters called the pharmacy board to encourage pursuit of the inquiry. He suggested a thorough examination of all the records of the Revco store most frequently used by the podiatrist. The pharmacy board got in touch with the Ohio Department of Public Welfare. Among the vast amounts of data stored on welfare department computer tapes were the prescription records of the targeted Revco store. As one of the state's largest Medicaid providers, Revco routinely sent records of all prescriptions filled for Medicaid recipients from its 159 pharmacies scattered around the state to corporate headquarters in Cleveland. There they were entered on tape and submitted to the welfare department as claims for reimbursement. The welfare department agreed to assist the pharmacy board by generating the computerized claims records for all Medicaid prescriptions written by the podiatrist and filled in the pinpointed store.

1

August 1976

Manual examination of the computer output began. An experienced analyst in the investigative unit of the welfare department, the Bureau of Surveillance and Utilization Review (SUR), further decomposed the data by hand, taking weeks to chronicle the prescription histories of forty-five patients of the podiatrist. This painstaking work exposed an irregularity. The prescription numbers did not flow in the usual ascending numerical order. Instead, lower prescription numbers occasionally occurred within a sequence of ascending numbers. Closer examination revealed that the last three digits of certain six-digit prescription numbers were being transposed. A pattern appeared. A prescription was recorded as a claim and three days later the identical prescription was recorded again with the last three digits transposed. This same pattern appeared in the hand-detailed report of each of the forty-five patients.

October 1976

To clarify whether the transposed prescription numbers were linked to the podiatrist's prescribing practice or to the Revco store, the pharmacy board and the welfare department's SUR agreed to expand the investigation. Computer-generated claims histories were ordered for twelve additional Revco stores in the same metropolitan area. Months passed as several SUR analysts examined the data manually. Transposed prescription numbers were found in each of the stores' computerized records, regardless of prescribing physician.

March 1977

A meeting was held between the welfare department's SUR and the pharmacy board to discuss possible explanations. The transposed prescription numbers could have been the result of a welfare computer mistake. To check this, claims histories were ordered for a different drug chain, in order to compare Revco's records with those of a competitor. There was a second possibility. The numbers could have been intentionally transposed by Revco. SUR and the pharmacy board suspected that certain prescriptions had been the basis of false billing to the welfare department, submitted for payment a second time with numbers transposed and dates changed. To test this alternative explanation, computer records of prescriptions with the transposed numbers would have to be verified against original prescriptions held in individual pharmacies. If the suspicious prescription numbers were indeed false, no matching originals would be found. If the suspicious prescriptions were authentic, the search would reveal originals that matched the computer printout in every detail.

This task had to be pursued without arousing suspicion. A mechanism existed that would accomplish it discreetly. The pharmacy board routinely sent investigators into licensed drug dispensing facilities around the state to examine records. A Revco store in a remote area of the state was chosen. An investigator who was familiar with it and whom the pharmacists knew personally was sent to do the job. Lists were prepared of sets of the suspect prescriptions. Each set consisted of a claim for a prescription with a specified number, and a claim for a second prescription identical to the first except for the transposed number and later date.

23 March 1977

Under the guise of a routine examination, the investigator visited the store. For the first prescription number in the set, he found a matching original. For the second, no matching original was found. The original that had the prescription number corresponding to the second number in the set bore a different patient name, drug type, and cost than those on the computer printout. The second prescription in each set was false. Revco apparently had been submitting the same prescription, with numbers transposed, for reimbursement a second time. The Ohio Department of Public Welfare had been reimbursing Revco for prescription claims through the Medicaid program. The question of whether a single podiatrist was practicing outside his area of specialization had led to the far wider possibility of Medicaid fraud by Revco, one of the largest drug retailers in the country, operating 825 stores in twenty-one states.[2] Revco had 159 stores in Ohio. How many of these stores were involved had yet to be determined.

The pharmacy board considered two possibilities: the false prescriptions could be the result of a conspiracy among several of the individual pharmacies—or they could have originated centrally, in the upper echelon of the corporate structure, thus af-

3

fecting every Revco store in the state. The board cast aside the notion of a conspiracy among employees at the store level, believing that the similarity of method across stores would have been unmanageable because of the numbers of people who would have to have been involved. Instead, the board concluded that the suspected fraud appeared to be a centrally originating computer crime, possibly statewide, conceived and carried out by a handful of people. Deciding that the case was bigger than it was prepared to handle, the board asked the Ohio State Highway Patrol to join the investigation because of its previous experience with welfare fraud cases and its statewide jurisdiction to investigate any criminal act involving state property interests.[3]

The next stage would be a delicate one. Every possible step must be taken to maintain secrecy, for Revco's awareness of the ongoing investigation might precipitate destruction of evidence. Further, the evidence must be secured in a manner that would both establish fraud and prevent any procedural errors that would provide Revco a loophole. On 11 April 1977, these contingencies led the highway patrol to ask the Economic Crime Unit of the Franklin County Prosecutor's Office—the county in which all welfare billing for the state originates—to enter the case. This unit assumed direction of the rest of the investigation, using its legal expertise to assure that no loopholes would occur.[4]

OBTAINING THE EVIDENCE

In order to charge Revco with fraud, the Economic Crime Unit needed sufficient evidence to establish probable cause. To do this, the unit had to prove that the corporation had been reimbursed by the welfare department for the false prescriptions, and to establish intent. First, the reimbursement problem. The computerized records of claims Revco had submitted to the welfare departments were examined. Fifteen sets of claims containing fifteen suspected fraudulent billings were traced and carefully compared with remittance statements and checks sent to Revco by the welfare department. The corporation had indeed received payment on each of the billings traced.[5]

Intent could be demonstrated by showing that the false prescriptions were in sufficient number to indicate that they had been generated knowingly and not as a result of negligence or mistake. The welfare department's Division of Data Services developed special computer programs to examine past claims paid to all Revco stores in the state. An interoffice memo reported the preliminary findings:

> This Bureau received and summarized a special computer report listing suspicious prescription numbers. We found that Revco Drug Stores, Inc., billing for 159 stores (100%) had used this same suspicious billing pattern for all stores. A peripheral concern is that Revco Drug Stores, Inc., of this state, bills centrally for 825 stores in 21 states. These 63,847 sets of suspicious prescription numbers represent a total cost to the Ohio Department of Public Welfare of $642,018.12 in historic payments.[6]

That the false prescriptions were occurring in every store in the state and that Revco had been reimbursed for a sample of the fraudulent billings were sufficient to establish probable cause. The stage was set for seizing the evidence.

A strategy was needed. Without access to the corporation, however, the investigators were at a disadvantage. The secrets of Revco's internal operations had to be reconstructed before the investigation could proceed, for any plan required knowledge of where in the organization the false prescriptions were originating, who was responsible, and how the billing was being manipulated. The Economic Crime Unit tried to learn as much about the company as possible. Through the welfare department, which had had transactions with Revco as a Medicaid provider since 1972, a picture of the corporate structure began to unfold. The unit consulted with the welfare department's Division of Data Services to learn the computer billing system for providers. From this inquiry, the Economic Crime Unit investigators were able to diagram the departments within Revco through which prescription claims normally passed. Working backwards through the claims submission process, a department within Revco was pinpointed from which the false billings might be originating.

Now certain that the fraud was occurring at corporate headquarters and having tentatively identified the point of origin, the Economic Crime Unit decided on its strategy. Original prescriptions would be seized simultaneously from several Revco pharmacies around the state. The original prescriptions, once in the possession of the investigating agencies, would provide a lever

5

to gain access to the internal structure of the corporation without risking destruction of evidence. Five stores in four counties were selected as targets. The stores were geographically scattered, both rural and urban, to protect against a legal defense that the act was a conspiracy between the stores rather than organization-wide. Yet simultaneous execution of search warrants in five locations in four counties was unprecedented. Planning and coordination were imperative. The Economic Crime Unit and the highway patrol together mapped the execution of the warrants, which would specify sets of suspicious prescriptions. Because of the findings of the pharmacy board's earlier on-site visit, the unit did not expect to find the originals of the prescriptions with the transposed numbers in the stores. Nonetheless, a large number of suspicious prescriptions had to be compared to originals to establish that the fraud was extensive.

The search warrants would be served in each pharmacy by a team composed of a highway patrol trooper, a representative of the local police, and a representative of the pharmacy board. The local police were included to cover any jurisdictional questions that might arise, the pharmacy board members because of their knowledge of store records. Staff at the welfare department, the highway patrol, and the Economic Crime Unit worked at night preparing the warrants, to conceal indications of the impending operation from insiders and outsiders alike. SUR and the Division of Data Services had painstakingly drawn up lists of the sets of suspect prescriptions in each of the five stores. The numbers of these 2,492 prescriptions had to be typed accurately into the warrants. To preserve secrecy, Revco's name was omitted from the warrants until the last possible minute. A local reporter whose regular beat was the county prosecutor's office was alerted by the extra activity. Picking Revco's name from a typed document, the reporter went to the prosecutor and threatened to make the operation public unless he was included. A bargain was struck: the reporter would be informed of the time and location of the search warrant executions in exchange for his silence until then. A one-day briefing session was conducted by the Economic Crime Unit for troopers from around the state who were participating, for any irregularity could mean a technical defense for Revco. Warrants were secured in each of the counties.

29 April 1977

A command post was set up between the Economic Crime Unit and the highway patrol to ensure simultaneous execution of the warrants. Highway patrol communication equipment was in readiness to keep in touch with the warrant execution. Unit staff were on duty to respond to any legal questions that might arise. The search warrant teams, assembled in scattered cities around the state waiting to begin, were in radio contact with the command post at all times.

9:00 to 9:45 A.M.

The search warrant teams entered the five Revco stores. Warrants were shown to the pharmacists on duty, the original prescriptions were seized, and inventory lists of those removed were left with the pharmacists. The seizure of the prescriptions went without incident, except for the appearence of press and photographers at one of the stores. At the entry of the search warrant teams, alarmed pharmacists notified corporate headquarters. Revco executives immediately telephoned the Economic Crime Unit. They were advised of the content of the warrants and the location of the five stores. When the execution of the warrants was completed, the unit contacted Revco's chairman of the board, scheduling a meeting for later that day.

12:00 noon.

Representatives of the welfare department's SUR, the highway patrol, and the Economic Crime Unit boarded a small plane and flew to meet corporate executives at the law offices of the chairman of the board in Cleveland, Ohio. As they left, headlines were already appearing in the local papers:

**REVCO WELFARE BILLING PROBED
N. High St. Store Searched
As Part of Four City Raid.**[7]

1:00 P.M.

Present at the meeting were Revco's chairman, the corporate legal counsel, and two attorneys from the law firm representing the corporation. The representatives of the investigative agencies informed corporate officials of the evidence. As the discovery of the false prescriptions was explained, the executives were shown computer printouts and detailed claims listings. They denied any knowledge of the false prescriptions. Two letters were delivered and accepted: a letter from the prosecutor's office requesting Revco's cooperation and listing the information the corporation was to supply, and a letter from the Ohio Department of Public Welfare informing Revco that payment on all claims would be suspended until completion of the investigation. Revco promised cooperation. The successful execution of the search warrants had won the combined investigative agencies the sought-after tactical advantage. Nearly a year had elapsed since the investigation began.

THE CORPORATE EXPLANATION

Within a matter of days, Revco confirmed its pledge to cooperate by hiring an independent auditing firm to perform an audit and assist in uncovering the billing problem. In addition, the chairman of the board responded in writing with the information requested by the Economic Crime Unit. On 13 May, a second meeting was held at Revco corporate headquarters. Present were representatives of the Economic Crime Unit, the highway patrol, the welfare department's data services, a representative of the auditing firm, and corporate officials. Revco stated that it had been conducting an internal investigation regarding the false claims. The parties responsible had been identified. Revco delivered a table of organization and names of staff in suspect positions to the patrol. Two troopers spent the next few days conducting interviews with current and former employees of the corporation. The interviews yielded an explanation of the false billings.

In the spring of 1975, corporate headquarters had moved to a new location. In the subsequent reorganization of departments, boxes of Medicaid claims were found. These claims, dating from 1973 to 1975, had been submitted to the welfare department for processing and reimbursement. However, the claims had been rejected by the Medicaid computer edits, special programs for prepayment screening of claims. The prepayment editing system screens claims for "errors," such as a charge of less than ten cents, date prescribed later than date dispensed, ineligible recipient, or disallowable drug. Rejected claims are sent back to the provider and reimbursement is withheld until the claim is corrected and successfully resubmitted. However, Revco personnel had not done the manual examination necessary to correct and resubmit the rejected claims. The rejects piled up. The prescription medication that the claims represented had been supplied to Medicaid recipients by Revco pharmacists. Hence, the boxes of rejected Medicaid claims signified outstanding accounts receivable. Over fifty thousand claims had been rejected by welfare department computers, representing over a half million dollars in accounts receivable.

Two Revco executives knew of these rejected claims and assumed responsibility for doing something about them. According to Revco officials, a vice-president and a program manager under his supervision embarked on a plan to bring the company's accounts receivable back into balance. To examine each claim individually and correct the errors legitimately would require personnel and time. The cost of correction would exceed the value of the claim. Therefore, a temporary clerical staff of six was hired specifically to work closely with the program manager and an assistant. Their sole responsibility was to alter the rejected claims so that they would be acceptable to the welfare department computer.

The vice-president and the manager possessed particular skills that enabled them to direct this project with minimal risk of detection by the welfare department computer system. The manager had formerly been director of Revco's computer system and was knowledgeable not only about Revco's own system, but about the welfare department computer billing and edit systems as well. The vice-president was a licensed pharmacist, knowledgeable about drugs and dosages. At their direction, new claims were fabricated. Clerical workers at corporate headquarters were instructed to manually rewrite claim forms in numbers equivalent to the rejected claims, rather than follow proper procedure for resubmissions to the state. They used "model claims"—claims which had already been accepted and paid by the state. Dates were changed, and the last three digits of the six digit prescription numbers were transposed. All other information from the model claims remained the same. No attempt was made to alter the amounts of the individual claims. The two executives believed

9

that because of the large number of claims involved, the amounts would average out. When the backlog of rejected claims had been rewritten and submitted to the welfare department, the temporary clerks were terminated. The plan devised in March 1975 was completed by December 1976. The two executives accepted total responsibility for the falsified claims, stating that their actions had been taken without the knowledge of any other persons employed by Revco. The state troopers interviewed the two executives and the clerical help. All confirmed the story.

Revco: Offender or Victim?

That Revco did indeed falsify prescriptions is indisputable. Yet at no time did the corporation admit to criminal behavior. In fact, throughout the case, in public statements and correspondence Revco assumed the role of the victim, not the offender. Corporate officials stated that a series of frustrating difficulties had occurred between Revco and the welfare department's Medicaid program since 1971. Revco placed the responsibility for these problems with the welfare department. A history of the interaction between the two organizations was recorded by Revco and presented in a memo to representatives of the prosecutor's office and the highway patrol.[8] Twenty-two incidents over a four-year period were listed to substantiate Revco's point that the corporation had repeatedly been victimized by the welfare department. The first entry, in November 1971, stated:

> We are informed by this date that there is a severe backlog of claims and that the state is about to run out of money for Medicaid. Communications during this period of time from this date [sic] were extremely poor. There were times when mailings were not made because the state lacked the necessary funds for postage.[9]

Welfare's initiation of a new computer billing system in 1972 was intended to resolve these reimbursement problems. Instead, according to Revco, increased confusion resulted. Difficulties such as system breakdown, claim backlogs, and infrequent reimbursement accompanied the phasing-in of the new system. Because of these transition dilemmas, the state was often behind in paying providers' claims.

The Revco memo listing Medicaid problems specifically mentioned rejected claims as early as 1974. In order to alleviate the rejection problem for Revco and other providers, the welfare department computer experts required major providers to install a presubmission edit system of their own to screen claims before sending them to the department for reimbursement. The intent was to catch errors in the claims so they could be corrected before the provider submitted them. This would reduce the number of claims rejected by welfare department computers. Revco was one of the providers that installed an edit system.

However, comparison of Revco's claims rejection rates with the rejection rates of other providers indicated that Revco's presubmission edit system was not functioning properly—errors were not being detected. The percentage of claims rejected by welfare department computers was higher for Revco than for other providers of similar size with similar screening systems. Average rejection rates for other providers varied from 2.0 percent to 6.0 percent per month, while a summary of Revco's claims indicated that from June 1976 to May 1977, an average of 24.04 percent of Revco's claims were being rejected. Indeed, the range of monthly rejections for the period was 5.4 percent to 56.3 percent.[10]

According to welfare department computer experts, the responsibility for this problem lay with Revco.[11] The company had been advised by the welfare department that its presubmission edit system was inadequately programmed, which was resulting in higher than average rejection rates. Although data services suggested changes in Revco's screening system that would reduce rejections, Revco did not make them. The reasoning behind this omission is not known to me. However, one might speculate that cost and complexity were relevant factors. The maintenance of a reliable presubmission edit system is expensive. Once installed, the provider's system requires constant adjustment, for the information needed by the welfare department frequently changes. Allowable claims vary. Recipient eligibility requirements may be altered. New drugs on the market necessitate constant revision of the drug formulary, a listing of disallowable drugs. A welfare department computer specialist, speaking of the Revco rejections, stated, "We complicate the problem by the amount of data we need."[12]

According to Revco officials, the executives responsible for the falsifications saw the rejected claims as another in a long line of inconveniences caused Revco by the welfare department. Prescriptions had been filled in "good faith."[13] Reimbursement was withheld. The rejects would be costly to correct, because of a "cold audit trail." Revco officials admitted that correction was theoretically possible, but not practical. The rejected claims were "rewritten" to "expedite the money the state owed us." Submitting false claims was seen as a solution to a "business problem," not as a crime.[14]

This "business problem" generated unlawful solutions in an additional way. Investigation by computer specialists from the welfare department's Division of Data Services disclosed that workers at Revco's corporate headquarters were told to "doctor up" claims rejected by the company's own presubmission edit system and send them through.[15] Thus, two types of false claims were discovered: claims rejected by welfare department computers were resubmitted with transposed numbers by clerks specifically hired to do the job, and claims rejected by Revco's own screening system were changed and resubmitted routinely by permanent Revco employees.

The welfare department's examination of prescription claims submitted for the 159 Revco pharmacies in Ohio revealed 208,539 disputed claims, for which Revco owed the state $521,521.12.[16] The combined efforts of the Economic Crime Unit, the Ohio Department of Public Welfare, the Ohio State Board of Pharmacy, and the Ohio State Highway Patrol had uncovered the largest case of Medicaid provider fraud in the state's history. Revco, the now admitted offender, was one of the largest retail drug chains in the state and in the nation. The disposition of the case proved to be as dramatic and complex as its discovery and investigation.

THE DISPOSITION OF THE CASE
Social, Economic, and Political Influences

Activity accelerated between the Economic Crime Unit and Revco as the case moved into the final stages. The outcome was not predicated simply upon the interaction between these two organizations, however. Instead, it reflected the matrix of social, economic, and political influences in which the negotiations were embedded.

Revco was under pressure for an early, quiet settlement and hoped to avoid a trial. The price of Revco's stock on the New York Stock Exchange had fallen rapidly at the time of the April raids. On 29 April, the day the prescriptions were seized, 67,800 shares of Revco stock were traded on the New York Stock Exchange. The price per share at closing was 20 3/4. One week later, the number of shares traded was 616,900. The closing price was 16 3/4. The stock price continued to vacillate, with volume of trading for a given week at times jumping to ten times the historic average for Revco.[17] Concern of major shareholders had been personally conveyed to members of the board of directors and other company officials. The fiscal year had ended 31 May 1977 and corporate officials expressed a wish to have the case settled as soon as possible—before the annual stockholders' meeting, scheduled for early September.

In addition, the evidence against Revco seemed convincing. A trial would mean continued unpredictability in the stock market and further bad publicity, not to mention cost in terms of company personnel involvement and legal fees. Corporate officials wanted to return to routine business, without the interruptions caused by the investigation. Internally, morale was low. The accused executives were long-time respected employees of the firm, and such events as sudden raids, headlines, and state troopers interviewing in corporate headquarters had a profound impact on all employees.[18] Moreover, the welfare department had suspended payment for Revco prescriptions to Medicaid recipients for the duration of the investigation. Revco, attempting to be cooperative and not wishing to lose customers, had continued to serve these Medicaid recipients. This backlog of unpaid billings was estimated to be $500,000.[19] Conclusion of the investigation, no matter what the outcome, would bring reimbursement for these claims.

The prosecutor's office also was interested in avoiding a trial and obtaining an early settlement. The size of the corporation and the amount and scope of the fraud had created national interest in the case. Financial analysts throughout the country repeatedly called for information to advise existing and potential stockholders, which caused those involved with the investigation to exercise extreme caution in all public utterances. Only in rare instances were statements issued to the press. Swift and quiet resolution was seen as beneficial to the general public—and to the prosecutor's office. Should the case go to trial, it would be lengthy, conceivably costing the county thousands of dollars. Jury selection for such a complex case must be done with care and would be time-consuming. Proving the case to a jury would be difficult, despite the amount of evidence. There would be many exhibits, Medicaid recipients would have to be called in to verify claims billed to them, and the case would of necessity rest upon the expert testimony of computer specialists.

Indeed, the prosecution had some concern about whether the evidence would stand up in court. First, the five stores selected for the prescription seizures were not randomly chosen. Since much of the later computer work was based on findings from the prescription records of these five stores, it may not have been generalizable. Second, the process by which the welfare department had arrived at the amount Revco owed them could be called into question. The welfare department had been confronted by the same problem of high cost of tracking errors which originally had led Revco to resort to falsification rather than correction. Hence the welfare department chose to quantify the loss by a stratified sample of claims extracted by ten specially devised computer programs, rather than locating each false prescription by manual examination and aggregating the cost. The stratified sampling process used was nonrandom and extracted claims on the basis of certain error types.[20] Valid claims may have been included in the sample.[21]

Because of these factors, a negotiated plea was mutually beneficial to Revco and the Economic Crime Unit. As negotiations were about to begin, however, the two organizations were influenced to hurry the bargaining by the attempted entry of the state attorney general's office in the case. The attorney general's office, though it had no jurisdiction,[22] initiated several meetings with Revco officials. Interviews and meeting notes confirmed that corporate officials were concerned about the possibility of civil suit by the attorney general as well as about the ongoing criminal prosecution by the county. As for the Economic Crime Unit, the attempted entry of the attorney general's office into the case created political pressure. Because the Revco case was the biggest case of Medicaid provider fraud that had occurred in the state and was receiving national publicity, the organization responsible for its successful resolution would receive good press and potential political rewards.

The Negotiated Plea

Formal meetings to discuss a plea began 29 June 1977 and continued for a month. The charges against the corporation and the two executives were negotiated simultaneously. As discussions got underway, the ramifications of negative publicity on the market were again brought home to Revco. On 7 July an imbalance in trading of Revco stock on the New York Stock Exchange halted trading of the issue. Speed of resolution and restoration of a positive public image became urgent.[23] Revco therefore agreed to waive its right to present the matter to the grand jury and proceed by way of information. An indictment meant a delay of two or three months while the case moved through the regular calendar; with a bill of information, a hearing would be scheduled within ten days of filing. In addition, newspapers report bills of information with much less vigor than indictments. For the Economic Crime Unit, concerned with speed, cost, and a successful resolution, a bill of information was also beneficial.

The Economic Crime Unit indicated two possible charges to Revco: theft by deception, a fourth degree felony, and falsification, a first degree misdemeanor.[24] Revco preferred the misdemeanor charge, for a felony charge raised the possibility of licensing suspension by pharmacy boards in several states, and would provoke greater negative public reaction. The misdemeanor offense was acceptable to the unit because it provided a greater penalty than the felony charges.[25] The unit proposed twenty counts of falsification, which would amount to a penalty fine of $100,000.

Because Revco owed the welfare department over a half million dollars, restitution was a priority in addition to whatever penalty might be imposed. However, the court could order restitution only if an offender was given probation, and probation was possible only with a felony charge.[26] Since a misdemeanor charge had been agreed upon, restitution would have to be obtained somehow through the plea negotiations. Although the welfare department did not participate in the negotiations, it played an important role in achieving this goal. The welfare department itself has the power to impose sanctions. The provider agreement can

15

be cancelled, resulting in termination of the provider's participation in the Medicaid program. When this occurs, Medicaid payment is not made for services rendered after the effective date of
termination.[27] Revco's annual Medicaid prescription sales in the
state at the time amounted to approximately $2 million, which
represented about 2 percent of the company's annual total sales
within the state.[28] Imposition of the termination sanction meant
a potential loss of this amount annually to Revco.

The welfare department eventually decided to retain Revco as
a Medicaid provider. Thousands of Medicaid recipients relied
upon Revco stores daily for prescriptions and service. Should
Revco's provider agreement be terminated, those recipients would
be forced to do business with another pharmacy. Such a transfer
would be in many cases an inconvenience and in others, a hardship. However, the announcement of this decision was left pend-
ing until the plea bargain was settled. This postponement presented
a tactical advantage to both the welfare department and the Economic Crime Unit. The absence of any public statement concerning termination left Revco uncertain about its future as a
provider. Thus, the potential application of this sanction was available for subtle use by the unit to gain restitution and ensure
cooperation in the plea bargain.

Ultimately, the negotiations were concluded with an agreement
that encompassed the following major elements: Revco agreed to
enter a plea of no contest to ten counts of falsification, a misdemeanor of the first degree. Under the organizational criminal
liability statute, the prosecution would recommend imposition of
the maximum fine of $5,000 per count.[29] This was agreed to by
Revco in consideration for proceeding by way of information. In
addition, Revco would make restitution in the amount of
$521,521.12 to the Ohio Department of Public Welfare.[30] As for
the two executives, each would plead no contest to two counts
of falsification. The prosecution would recommend imposition of
the maximum fine for a first degree misdemeanor provided by the
statute defining personal accountability for organizational conduct, $1,000 for each of two counts.[31] The charges also carried a
possible six-month jail sentence per count. Because the two executives derived no personal enrichment through their conduct,
the prosecutor's office agreed to make no recommendation as to
restitution or incarceration.

On 29 July 1977, representatives of the prosecutor's office gathered in the Franklin County Court of Common Pleas. The Revco vice-president and the manager were present, each accompanied by an attorney. No other corporate officers were present. Revco itself was represented by an attorney. The counsel for the state and counsels for the defendants placed upon the record the negotiated plea agreement encompassing all agreements between the parties. The defendants, in writing, entered their pleas of "no contest" to charges of falsification, as agreed. The counsel for the county presented the facts of the case to the court, which found the defendants guilty of each count, as charged. They were sentenced according to the negotiated plea agreement. That same afternoon Revco turned over checks for $521,521.12 and $50,000 to the Ohio Department of Public Welfare and the prosecutor's office, respectively. The two executives each rendered payments of $2,000 to the state. The largest case of Medicaid provider fraud in the state was officially closed.

Headlines reported the conclusion of the case: "Revco Stores, Two Officials Found Guilty"; "Revco Convicted of Using False Billings to Collect on Ohio Medicaid Prescriptions."[32] Yet questions linger. For some, there are answers. The program manager who participated in the creation of the false prescription claims received a lateral transfer to another department in Revco headquarters. The vice-president resigned from the company prior to the stockholders' meeting in September 1977, later accepting a position as vice-president of a corporation which provides computer services to pharmacies. As for the podiatrist whose suspected criminal activity triggered the Revco investigation—at this writing his case is still open. When the Revco case first appeared in the newspapers, his peculiar prescribing practices ceased and good evidence has never been obtained.

As for Revco, the company revamped its billing system by installing special computer preedits as required by the welfare department. A better interface between the two systems resulted. The welfare department adjusted its own claims screening system by devising several new computer programs to detect claims submitted with transposed prescription numbers. In addition, all future Revco claims would be closely scrutinized for an indeterminate period. Revco was given the opportunity to correct and resubmit all claims that had been falsified. In a letter dated 24 October 1977 from the vice-president of systems at Revco to the head of the welfare department's data services, the corporation's position was stated:

> After studying the amount of labor involved in pulling the original claim form and matching it to the reject listings, it was decided that the cost of reprocessing would be too high to make that reprocessing economically feasible. All of the efforts that would be required to work on these old claims would be diverted from our current claims and result in a continuing backlog. We have decided to devote our processing efforts to fresh claims.[33]

Nearly five years later, in April 1981, Revco's application to have its criminal record expunged was granted by the Court of Common Pleas, Franklin County, Ohio.[34] The court concluded that this was a first offense, that Revco had no subsequent criminal proceedings against it, and that the corporation's rehabilitation had been attained. The court declared, therefore, that it was consistent with the public interest to remove Revco's offense from the public record. This is the first time that an expungement statute, created for individual first offenders, had been applied to an organization.[35]

Other questions remain which may never be resolved. When the backlog of rejected claims was first discovered, why did Revco not attempt to negotiate with the welfare department about the reimbursement problem? Moreover, numerical transpositions are a common fraudulent technique. Why would corporate executives use such an unsophisticated method, especially in Ohio, where the welfare department has one of the most elaborate computer systems of any department in the country? And why would Revco go to the expense of hiring clerks to rewrite the claims? Was this any less costly than legitimate correction would have been? Why were these same clerks not used to correct the rejected and unreimbursed claims? Indeed, is it possible that six temporary clerks could be hired in one department for twenty-one months and their presence and function not be questioned? Is it possible that there could be $500,000 outstanding accounts receivable and the corporate hierarchy not be aware of the fact? And finally, the Revco vice-president who early in the case called the pharmacy board to urge analysis of store records regarding the podiatrist was the same vice-president who admitted collaborating on the creation of the false prescriptions. If he knew there were prescription claims that were not authentic, why had he encouraged the investigation? These questions all relate to what lawyers call "the facts of the case." For the sociologist, interest goes beyond the missing pieces of the investigative puzzle to focus on the Revco case as a particular form of unlawful behavior, in which both victim and offender are complex organizations. For the sociologist, then, the lingering questions are of a different nature, a broader scale. Two will be addressed. First, how, in this case, did society organize to combat unlawful organizational behavior? Second, in what ways is society organized that may encourage the very phenomenon it seeks to control?

2

The Social
Control
Network

The control of unlawful organizational behavior is an issue of increasing relevance. Although the organization of the control environment is a critical consideration, seldom has the topic been broached empirically.[1] The Revco investigation presents an opportunity to examine, sociologically, the response to a particular case of organizational misconduct by five investigative agencies which worked together on the case, forming a social control network. The major concern is to identify the crucial characteristics of this network and construct a conceptual model of a functioning system. This will, in a sense, be an exercise in typology.[2] This structure is the first of its kind to be explored. It may turn out to be a member of a class of similar objects, or it may be that the class has only one member.[3] Whichever is true, identification of the defining characteristics of this model is a necessary first step. Once defined, the model can be tested by determining whether its relevant features are found in other organizational forms.

NETWORK EMERGENCE

As has been noted, a number of organizations actively participated in the Revco investigation: the Ohio State Board of Pharmacy, the Ohio Department of Public Welfare, the Ohio State Highway Patrol, and the Economic Crime Unit of the Franklin County Prosecutor's Office. Within the welfare department, the investigation was handled by two specialized subunits, the Bureau of Surveillance and Utilization Review (SUR), and the Division of Data Services. Both these subunits represented the interests of the larger organization. For analytical purposes, however, they will be treated as if they were separate organizations. Consequently, the analysis will focus on five organizations: the pharmacy board, SUR, data services, the highway patrol, and the Economic Crime Unit. Because these organizations were directly involved in the investigation, they are identified as *primary* organizations. Two other organizations were indirectly involved in the case: the Office of State Auditor and the Office of State Attorney General. Although they did not participate in the investigation, they later influenced the structure and functioning of the organizational network and are necessary to the analysis. Because of their indirect involvement, they are identified as *peripheral* organizations. Of these seven organizations, six were state agencies; only the Economic Crime Unit was a county organization. However, all were located in the same city: Columbus, Ohio. All were investigative organizations in their own right with resources which could be brought to bear on violators of agency regulations or law. Investigative technology varied, tailored to the specific tasks for which each agency was designed. All but two had sanctions available to reinforce compliance. The seven organizations were created by law, with domains defined by law.

Two limitations should be noted. While each of these organizations routinely dealt with many others, activities with organizations other than the ones participating in the Revco investigation will be ignored. Second, each of these organizations has highly complex domains.[4] To describe all of their separate goals and functions would be confusing, rather than enriching. Therefore, only those aspects that are relevant to the Revco case are presented.

Conditions for Network Formation

Cooperation between organizations is known to be encouraged by corresponding ideologies, as well as by domain consensus—a set of stable expectations about what an organization will or will not do.[5] Furthermore, evidence suggests that emergent groups tend to develop around previous interaction patterns, which provide the basis for further structural differentiation and organizational development.[6] Indeed, these factors contributed to network formation in the Revco investigation. Linkages existed between these agencies prior to the surfacing of Revco's suspected fraud. A linkage is any recurrent pattern of behavior, purposive and stable, which exists between two systems and is supported by both of the systems—in other words, a mutual benefit relationship.[7] These linkages grew out of the need for resources to improve agency capabilities. For example, the highway patrol regularly used the Economic Crime Unit's legal knowledge by asking the unit to assess a case under investigation, to insure adequate preparation for prosecution. In exchange, the patrol frequently served as an additional investigative tool for the unit.

All seven organizations, moreover, were commonweal organizations charged with protecting the public interest. Although they represented various governmental units (state and county), each performed social control functions. Thus, they shared a policing ideology. Finally, because they were all commonweal organizations, the domain of each was defined by law. This public definition of these organizations' goals and functions facilitated agreement and understanding, both for members and for others with whom they interacted, about the organizations' responsibilities and how they would be fulfilled (see table 1).[8]

Thus, the seven organizations were not strangers prior to the Revco case. Corresponding ideologies, domain consensus, and past linkages between them laid the groundwork for a collaborative effort. Yet a point should be stressed about their previous association: never had more than two organizations combined resources toward the control of a single suspected violator. What, then, triggered their joint participation in the Revco investigation?

A Focused Network

Interviews and interorganizational memos indicated three factors precipitated the direct involvement of five organizations:
1. Task Complexity: The suspected offender was a complex organization with millions of dollars in assets, thousands of employees, and locations throughout the state and nation. Although the several organizations had experience investigating Medicaid fraud, never had they faced a case with so large a corporation as the suspect, nor such potentially extensive fraud and dollar loss.
2. Uncertainty: In the Revco investigation, uncertainty occurred when (a) the task was not clear, (b) the organizational domain in which the task fell was not clear, (c) the technology was not clear, or (d) resource exchange was necessary for task completion. Frequently, routine patterns of investigation were in-

adequate. Questions arose concerning task, domain, technology, or resources. "How do you sneak up on a corporation!"—a statement made several times during interviews—underscored the uncertainty of the situation.

3. Specialization: Each of the organizations participating in the investigation possessed resources separate and distinct from those of the others. The concept "resources" as it is used here includes organizational sanctions, physical facilities and equipment, aggregate skills and competencies, information and knowledge.[9]

As a consequence of the nature of the offense, the offender, and their own specialization, none of the agencies was able to complete the investigation independent of the resources of the others: all five were necessary to the network.[10]

Interestingly, their joint effort closely adheres to the characteristics of a focused network, a concept developed to describe the reaction of community organizations to mass casualty situations.[11] In the absence of coordinated expertise, numbers of separate organizations focus upon accomplishing a specific social task. As the complexity of the task increases, so does the need for a complex resource base, and a multiple organization response is found more often. This response is called a focused network because of the specific social task, or focus, toward which the organizations direct their attention, and because of the absence of coherence in the group effort. Absence of coherence or wholeness is a characteristic which distinguishes a network from a social system:

> Networks are not limited to a structure of linkages, but based on a set of units and the pattern of linkages between them. Between any two units, no link is necessary, and, in fact, a unit may have no links at all with other units, while still being considered as part of the social network. The emphasis is then upon patterns of relationships between units rather than the tracing of linkages alone.[12]

Although the response of organizations in mass casualty situations is immediate while the response in the Revco case was sequential rather than simultaneous, the notion of a focused network describes both situations well enough to suggest its utility in analyzing multiple organizations responding to complex deviant

TABLE 1: Description of Organizations Relevant to the Revco Case

	Level	Organizational Domain
Primary Organizations		
Ohio State Board of Pharmacy	State	Secures compliance with and enforcement of drug laws related to dispensers of drugs: compliance is sought by spreading knowledge of drug laws and enforcement activities to individual dispensing facilities; enforcement by inspection and licensing of drug facilities.
Ohio Department of Public Welfare: Bureau of Surveillance and Utilization Review (SUR)	State	Guards against fraud and abuse of Medicaid program by its individual providers and recipients. Monitors and controls level of Medicaid care delivered to Medicaid recipients. Recovers funds lost to the state through misuse of the system, both by providers and recipients.
Ohio Department of Public Welfare: Division of Data Services	State	Uses computer facilities to identify providers and areas of their practice where possible overutilization of the Medicaid program may exist. Also, develops computer programs to quantify losses to Medicaid program. Interacts with providers to educate for improved system use.
Ohio State Highway Patrol	State	Investigates any criminal act on state-owned property. Also, pursues any criminal investigation which involves state property interests.
Franklin County Prosecutor's Office: Economic Crime Unit	County	Prepares and prosecutes cases of fraud, embezzlement, and other forms of white-collar crime for Franklin County, Ohio.
Peripheral Organizations		
Office of State Auditor	State	Ascertains that all payments made by the state are legal by auditing all claims through computer and manual review. Discovers and investigates fraud against the state.
Office of State Attorney General	State	Prepares cases, brings suit, and prosecutes on behalf of the state and all its departments. Has civil powers in cases in which state is a party or has a direct interest. At time of Revco case, criminal powers were restricted to cases of organized crime.

Specialization	Sanctions	Number of Organizational Linkages Prior to Revco Investigation
Surveillance, Investigation	Yes	4
Surveillance, Investigation	Yes	5
Surveillance, Investigation, Computer Facilities	No	5
Investigation	Yes	5
Investigation, Prosecution	Yes	2
Surveillance, Investigation, Computer Facilities	No	4
Investigation, Prosecution	Yes	5

events. The unique aspects of the Revco case—the characteristics of victim and offender, the nature of the illegal behavior, the amount of the loss—combined to produce an event not only unprecedented in the state's Medicaid fraud investigation history, but also unexpected, as a disaster is often unprecedented and unexpected. (The term "unexpected," as used here, refers to the absence of an organized system to deal with an event when it occurs.) And, as in disasters when no organized system exists to react, multiple organizations responded to the event. The complexity of the task of investigating Revco's suspected fraud and the corresponding need for a complex resource base were evident. Further, examination of linkages between network organizations throughout the investigation revealed that not all units formed links with all other units, therefore meeting the noncoherence criterion of a focused network. (The Economic Crime Unit, for example, did not directly interact with the pharmacy board at any time during the investigation, nor had it previously done so.)[13]

The two peripheral organizations associated with the case served functions and possessed resources nearly identical to two of the organizations that became primary members of the focused network. Why were some organizations included as primary participants while others were relegated to peripheral roles? The state auditor's office, possessing its own computerized records of Medicaid claims and a team of skilled investigators, could have performed the functions carried out by the welfare department's SUR and data services. The state attorney general's office, with legal expertise and prosecution powers, could have assumed the role played in the investigation by the county's Economic Crime Unit. Interviews indicate that the decision to include or exclude an organization was based on (1) the perceived immediate needs of the investigation, (2) specialization, and (3) pre-existing linkages with the decision-making organization.

The duration of the Revco investigation was fifteen months; the selection of participating organizations was spread over eleven months (see table 2). The decision-making authority was the organization that had control of the case at the time. When two organizations were qualified to meet the anticipated needs of the investigation, the one chosen had the resources and skills most appropriate for a Medicaid fraud investigation in the pharmacy industry which involved a large loss and a corporate offender.

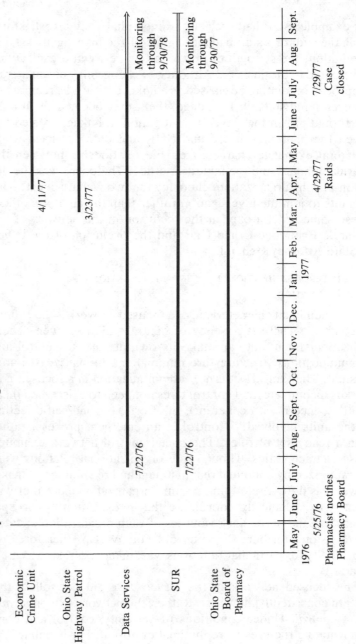

TABLE 2: Length of Participation of Network Organizations

For example, SUR had specially trained pharmacy investigators, while the auditor's staff had more generalized investigative skills. In addition, the strength of previous ties between organizations contributed to the decision. Although exchange may be unilateral, reciprocal, or joint, to be classed as a linkage it must be reciprocal, recurrent, and stable.[14] Exchange, then, may occur without linkage formation. In the Revco investigation, a linkage existed between the pharmacy board and SUR and data services, while unilateral exchange characterized the relationship between the pharmacy board and the auditor's office. The board was the decision-making organization, choosing the two welfare department subunits to join the investigation rather than the auditor's office. These same criteria explain the inclusion in the network of the county's Economic Crime Unit and the exclusion of the Office of State Attorney General.[15]

INTERORGANIZATIONAL NETWORK RELATIONS
Integration

A dominant characteristic of a focused network is the pattern of control.[16] There is absence of centralization or even decentralization. Each unit can make its own decisions. Control and communications structures are minimal and in many cases nonexistent. The typical pattern of communication in a focused network is incomplete, and control does not need to exist when there is little concern with coherence of efforts, beyond self-direction of the units involved.[17] Control is an emergent process, rather than a ready set of rules. The social control network exhibited these characteristics. Though interorganizational relations were characterized by continual readjustment and redefinition of tasks, power was diffuse. No "linking pin" organization existed or was created to specifically coordinate the investigation.[18] The specialization and particular resources of each organization dictated the division of labor. Domains did not overlap; therefore, responsibility for particular functions was, in most cases, extremely clear.

The focused network in the Revco case did not follow this pattern consistently, however. Rather, the network exhibited *sporadic control*. Under conditions of certainty, control and communication structures were minimal or absent. For example, the pharmacy board's initial request for information about a podiatrist who was apparently prescribing outside his area of specialization led data services to produce a claims history and SUR to do an analysis—both routine tasks—completed autonomously. Under conditions of certainty, the separate organizations pursued their tasks in this manner, with minimal and informal communication. Under conditions of uncertainty, control and communication structures increased, and one of the network organizations became dominant over one or more of the others. The organization assuming control was the one in whose domain the problem most clearly lay. No single organization consistently assumed control; rather, the dominant organization varied with the task at hand.

The relationship between uncertainty and increased control and communication in the network is illustrated by the execution of the search warrants. The Economic Crime Unit was confronted with the problem of executing the warrants simultaneously in five locations around the state. There was uncertainty about jurisdiction, the form of the affidavits, the form of the warrants, and the personnel to execute them. The unit assumed responsibility for this phase of the case because of its specialized knowledge of the technical requirements necessary for evidence to hold up in court. The unit then directed and coordinated the efforts of the highway patrol, SUR, and data services throughout the planning, preparation, and execution stages. Uncertainty precipitated resource exchange and increased and formalized communications, and, as noted, one organization assumed dominance and control over the others.

The appearance of sporadic control underscores the variability in degree of network integration during the Revco investigation. Conditions of uncertainty precipitated periods in which some or all of the separate organizations became more tightly integrated. However, for the most part, network integration could be described as loosely coupled: the investigative agencies retained their identity and their physical and logical separateness, even though they were responsive to one another.[19] A question frequently raised concerning a single organization consisting of separate units that are loosely coupled is, what holds the organization together?[20] The same question deserves consideration when the phenomenon under investigation is a loosely coupled network of organizations. Though the network organizations continued to exist as autonomous entities, pursuing their individual and sometimes conflicting goals throughout the duration of the Revco case, the common goal of solving the case bound the several organizations together. In other words, the *focus* of a focused network plays a major part in its integration, as well as its emergence.[21] Two other factors contributed to the integration of this network: the shared policing ideologies of the separate organizations and the need for resource exchange.

Cooperation, Competition, and Conflict

Because each network organization possessed resources which were necessary to the investigation, many network activities were voluntary and cooperative. This cooperation is best illustrated by the mutual socialization that occurred between network organizations. For example, data services' representatives spent many hours meeting with the other organizations to explain the numerical codes of the Medicaid system so that the evidence could be collected, recorded, interpreted, and explained in court, if the case proceeded to that point. Another example was the Economic Crime Unit's rigorous training of the highway patrol troopers in proper search warrant execution, necessary because of the multiple jurisdictions involved. Though interorganizational relations were mainly cooperative, competition and conflict also were present: competition for resources outside the network and conflict among the organizations regarding the sanctions imposed.

Competition for good press occurred among the network organizations. Publicity was important to all the organizations because they were competing with other governmental units for funds and wished their accomplishments to be known. All press releases concerning the Revco case were issued by the Economic Crime Unit, but because of the need to maintain secrecy, no press releases were issued until after the seizure of the prescriptions. Thus, the publicity gave information on the facts of the case from that point on. The early stages of discovery and investigation were not reported to the public, concealing the contribution to the investigation made by the welfare department's SUR, data services, and the pharmacy board. In interviews in these three network organizations, members complained that their agency did not get the deserved press recognition.

Conflict arose because of the sanctions imposed on Revco. The focus of the network gave all the organizations a common goal:

social control of Revco Drug Stores, Inc. Although this general goal was shared, individually the organizations disagreed on the proper sanctions. The sanctions were the outcome of plea negotiations between the Economic Crime Unit and Revco. Because the other network organizations were not included in the bargaining, they were unaware of the barriers to sanctioning the unit confronted.[22] Though restitution of the amount owed the Ohio Department of Public Welfare was applauded by all organizations, the unit was accused of "giving the case away" because of the misdemeanor charges, bill of information, no contest plea, and amount of the fine.[23]

Litwak and Hylton note that conflict between organizations is taken-for-granted in interorganizational analysis and assume that a situation of partial conflict always exists.[24] The task of the sociologist, then, is to examine the forms of social interaction that occur under these circumstances. In the Revco case, the extent to which cooperation, competition, and conflict existed among the network organizations fluctuated over time.[25] Network activities were characterized by cooperation during the discovery and investigation stages, but competition and conflict appeared after the case became public knowledge. Sumner defined the tension produced by simultaneous existence of cooperative and competitive relations as antagonistic cooperation.[26] Indeed, antagonistic cooperation seems an ideal description of network relations.

NETWORK ASSESSMENT

How did network formation affect the execution of the Revco investigation? The agencies benefited from increased resources, flexibility, and mutual socialization. The joint effort expanded the resource base to include computer facilities and knowledge; access to pharmacy records; knowledge of drugs; investigative skills; expansion of jurisdiction, authority, and personnel to execute search warrants; clerical help; and legal knowledge. In addition, several of the organizations had their own sanctions, increasing the sanctioning capabilities of the network. The flexibility of the network also aided in the investigation. The absence of centralized control and pre-established investigation routines created a fertile environment for innovation. As a consequence, network operations were particularly designed to suit the suspected offender. The strategy for the search warrant execution is but one example.

Another advantage was mutual socialization, which expanded the knowledge of each agency. The shared creation of new solutions for confronting unlawful organizational behavior plus the awareness of the other organizations' resources and personnel better prepared each network organization to confront this type of offense and offender in the future, and better prepared them to interact with each other.

One problem that accompanied network formation was occasional duplication of effort. For example, the highway patrol and SUR separately made detailed records of the false prescriptions. Weeks of work were involved. This duplication occurred because, despite the existence of the network and the common focus, each organization retained its autonomy and therefore its separate goals and functions throughout the investigation. The welfare department's SUR recorded prescriptions to quantify the amount owed the welfare department. The highway patrol recorded prescriptions to prepare and gather evidence for the trial. In pursuit of two separate ends, the task was duplicated. Yet whether this duplication was a problem or an advantage is arguable, hinging on whether the incident is framed as a question of efficiency or of effectiveness. Whenever multiple demands exist for particular resources, the expenditure of time and talent to do a task twice is inefficient. Nonetheless, had the Revco case gone to trial, documentation of the false prescriptions by two separate organizations would have presented a stronger case from an evidentiary standpoint.[27]

Another and perhaps more critical instance of duplicated effort occurred in the late stages of investigation. The Economic Crime Unit spent considerable time and effort trying to piece together information that would reveal how the violation was committed and where in the Revco organization it had occurred. Interviews disclosed that this same information had been uncovered earlier in the case by the Ohio State Board of Pharmacy through the use of an informant. Somehow, the solution to the puzzle had never been relayed to the prosecutor's office. This omission may be explained by the timing of the participation of these two organizations in the investigation, their separate tasks, and the absence of previous exchange between them. Examination of the linkages between network organizations indicated no interaction previous to the Revco case between the pharmacy board and the unit.

Moreover, the major work of the pharmacy board was at the point of discovery and later in gaining access to individual pharmacy records. By the time the Economic Crime Unit was brought in to prepare the case for trial, the pharmacy board had completed its undercover activity (see table 2). Thus, the two organizations never had the opportunity to interact.

The problems noted, however, should not be taken as a natural accompaniment to a focused network response to organizational illegality. They may simply have been a function of what Stinchcombe calls the liability of newness.[28] He points out that the relative weakness of newer social structure has four sources: (1) the necessity to learn new roles, (2) the absence of standard social routines, (3) the necessity to rely heavily on social relations among strangers, and (4) others' lack of familiarity with organizational services.[29] In the social control network under consideration, these four factors were apparent in interorganizational relations. One might speculate that subsequent joint efforts may have proceeded with increased efficiency, as a result of the mutual socialization processes.

AFTERMATH: THE POLITICS OF ENFORCEMENT

The efficiency of the social control network in future investigations must remain in the realm of speculation, however. When the case was closed, the network organizations returned to their separate responsibilities. Soon after, political reaction led by the two peripheral organizations resulted in changes that eliminated the possibility that the network would ever exist again in the form that evolved to investigate Revco's misconduct. Once the resolution of the case appeared in the newspapers, the Economic Crime Unit and the welfare department were publicly criticized by representatives of the Offices of State Auditor and State Attorney General for the sanctions imposed: not only for the amount of the fine, but also for the failure to terminate Revco as a Medicaid provider.[30] What followed must be understood within the then existing political situation. The Revco investigation concluded in an election year. The director of the Department of Public Welfare, a political appointee, and the county prosecutor, were Republicans. Both peripheral organizations were administered by Democratic officials. The incumbent county prosecutor (R) and the incumbent attorney general (D) had both declared themselves as candidates for the Office of State Attorney General in the forthcoming statewide election.

The auditor's office (D) was responsible for a number of press releases which criticized the sanctions in the Revco case. In response to this publicity, four bills which provided increased penalties for Medicaid providers who violated the law were introduced by Democratic legislators in the Ohio legislature. Among these bills was Ohio HB 159, initiated and developed by the Office of Attorney General. In addition to providing increased penalties for Medicaid providers who participated in a fraud, HB 159 allocated statewide criminal prosecution powers to the attorney general in such cases. Previously, criminal prosecution powers were delegated to county prosecutors and the attorney general was limited to civil suit.[31] The political significance of the new bill was that the attorney general's office would gain the right to prosecute both civilly and criminally, as well as the right to choose the cases that office would pursue. The others would be referred to the county.[32] Moreover, the acquisition of criminal prosecution powers by the attorney general's office qualified that office to receive 90 percent federal funding to form a State Medicaid Fraud Control Unit.[33]

The bill conferring the important criminal prosecution powers upon the attorney general's office was signed into law in April 1978—almost a year to the day after the raids on the five Revco drug stores. Granted three years of federal support, a new State Medicaid Fraud Control Unit was formed. Exclusively designed to prosecute providers, the new unit was supported by a contractual agreement with the Ohio Department of Public Welfare, which stated that all evidence would be turned over to the state, rather than the county.

In short, the two peripheral organizations, the state auditor's office and the attorney general's office, were in conflict with primary network organizations. This conflict was politically based. The consequence was expansion of domain by the attorney general's office by incorporation of external resources. The attorney general's office first laid the legislative groundwork, then obtained funding from the federal government to create a State Medicaid Fraud Control Unit.[34] For the social control network, the repercussions were deep. This new state unit usurped the role of the single county network organization, the Economic Crime Unit, in the prosecution of Medicaid provider fraud. Hence, the future discovery, investigation, and prosecution of important Medicaid provider fraud cases would be conducted entirely by state agencies. Moreover, this change in network structure—the inclusion of the State Medicaid Fraud Control Unit—was supported by a contractual agreement as well as by federal law. The network, which originally had emerged spontaneously and was based on unwritten agreements, had developed a linkage between organizations that was formalized. A very real and immediate loss was the base of knowledge, linkages, and experience developed between the network organizations over the course of the investigation, which might have enhanced network operations in investigating future cases of Medicaid provider fraud in the pharmacy industry had the network persisted unchanged. Whether the legislated changes enacted after the conclusion of the Revco case resulted in benefits or costs in the long run is beyond the scope of this research.

THEORETICAL AND PRACTICAL IMPLICATIONS

Despite the lack of generalizability of findings in any case study, the network response in the Revco investigation raises interesting issues of both a theoretical and practical nature. Theoretically, the emergence of the social control network calls into play both the conflict and functionalist paradigms. The conflict paradigm seems to explain not only the emergence of the network, but also the highly cooperative interaction patterns and the form the network took. When confronted by a common enemy, persons and groups may be brought together around a singular aim, and when the effort either succeeds or fails, they go back to the former separate existence.[35] The social control network was a fleeting organizational form composed of separate units joined together by their adversarial relationship with Revco. The conflict not only was the reason for group formation, but acted as an integrative force, linking the organizations together until the case was concluded. Throughout the undercover investigation, cooperation was strong. Only after Revco was confronted with the evidence and the case became public did competition and conflict occur. With the conclusion of the investigation, the organizations again pursued their independent goals, thus completing the life cycle of the network.[36]

35

Groups in conflict tend to mirror the form of the opponent, in order to minimize the advantages of the adversary.[37] Although the network organizations could not exactly simulate the structure of the corporation, they did, by banding together, increase their complexity. But most important, the unification expanded their resource base, decreasing their competitive disadvantage and increasing both effectiveness and efficiency. Isomorphism refers to a set of interorganizational processes that make organizations look more alike.[38] Conflict, and surely competition as well, deserve further study as isomorphic processes that increase homogeneity between organizations.

The functionalist paradigm seems to explain the selection of organizations into the network.[39] Notwithstanding the distinction between a system and a network made earlier, certain structures were indispensable to the network in meeting its goal. Each organization was chosen to fulfill a specific purpose for which specialization made it particularly suited. No overlap or duplication of resources existed among network organizations. The evidence confirms that alternative structures exist to fulfill basic requisites, for the peripheral organizations were sufficiently specialized to meet the demands of the investigation.[40] The data document the specific processes by which each organization was selected to participate in the network, as well as the criteria for selecting one over another when two were similarly qualified to meet network needs. The organizations were sifted and sorted on the basis of which *best* met network needs—some assigned to peripheral roles in the investigation as others with more appropriate resources and stronger ties were included as primary network organizations.

The practical implications concern the network as an effective device for social control. The emergence of multiple regulatory agencies is a fact of our time. Because no single organization has developed the capability to pursue all the various kinds of unlawful organizational behavior, regulatory agencies have proliferated, each with expertise in a specific area. Despite this development, the changing nature of organizational illegality requires such specialized knowledge and investigative skills that resource exchange between agencies seems a useful strategy. Resources of individual investigative agencies, such as jurisdictional powers, computer knowledge and technology, access to crucial records, or even arrest powers can be brought into an investigation at a telling moment. Then, when no longer needed, each organization can invest its energies and resources elsewhere. Since no single organization can be expected to develop the proficiency to resolve all types of unlawful organizational behavior, a focused network response allows use of existing specialization to maximum advantage. Another unique advantage of a network response is the flexibility afforded—the dynamicity, the ability of organizations to band together and disband as needed. Indeed, this is one of the more remarkable findings of this study, for research repeatedly has confirmed the inflexibility of bureaucracy.[41] Yet in the Revco case five agencies acted together to create a new organizational form which allowed innovation and flexibility, while still preserving the individual structure of each organization.

Despite these apparent practical benefits, some caveats concerning the potential effectiveness of networks as social control mechanisms must be considered. First, the cooperation among agencies exhibited in the Revco investigation may be an idiosyncratic finding. Typically, relations among regulatory agencies may be characterized by the insularity problem: the secrecy surrounding an investigation, competition for government funds, unwillingness to admit a need for outside help, or lack of information about the resource potential of other agencies may inhibit network formation.[42] Remember that the organizations in this case study were state and local, not federal. An interesting topic for future research would be examination of the circumstances under which a social control network does or does not form as a response to a suspected case of unlawful organizational behavior.

Second, a network response to some complex deviant event is likely to result in a temporary organizational form. The network that developed in the Revco case was a social creation in response to a specific problem. The fact that a network formed and accomplished a task does not mean that a mechanism for controlling organizational misconduct exists now where none existed before, however. This network emerged because of a common focus which dictated the necessary resources and, as a consequence, the organizations that would participate. Regardless of the intervention of legislative authority which precluded the network from responding similarly to future cases, the completion of the Revco case still would have resulted in the demise of the network. Moreover, the response was to an event with unique characteristics:

Medicaid provider fraud in the pharmacy industry. For another type of violation, the network's developed skills and even some of the organizations that participated become inappropriate.

Third, this particular network emerged because the social control agencies were unequal to the corporation they were investigating in both resources and public reputation. They were adversaries at opposite ends of the organizational stratification system. This competitive disadvantage was reduced by the pooling of resources to investigate the case. However, the suspected offender is not always a large and wealthy corporation. The competitive disadvantage may instead rest with the small business firm.[43] Use of networks to expand the resources of public agencies must be accompanied by creative restraints that protect small businesses from the burden of overregulation. For in the long run, the citizenry may be as concerned with controlling the behavior of a large and powerful government as with controlling the behavior of the giant corporation—for both have the potential to engage in unlawful conduct.

Fourth, and perhaps most important, is the question of the effectiveness of a network response in sanctioning and controlling unlawful organizational behavior. This topic is addressed in the next chapter.

Sanctioning the
Corporation

The organizations participating in the social control network were each included because they possessed resources that were critical to the investigation. Because the organizations were investigative agencies in their own right, several had sanctions available to reinforce compliance. Thus, as organizations were added, the network inadvertently gained resources that could be used in sanctioning the suspected offender, should the case proceed to that stage. Specifically, the Ohio State Board of Pharmacy, with legislatively based authority to enforce drug laws related to dispensers of drugs, could initiate mandatory license revocation should a violation result in criminal prosecution through the courts and a felony conviction be the consequence. In addition, the welfare department could terminate a provider from participation in the Medicaid program if efforts to secure compliance with regulations failed or if fraud were established.

The sanctions of these two organizations, however, were not imposed upon Revco: the corporation's license to distribute drugs was not revoked, nor was the Medicaid provider contract terminated. Though the participation of multiple organizations increased the potential sanctioning power of the network, the final sanctions did not reflect the range available. Given that the sociological explanation offered in chapter 2 for the focused network response included the need for an expanded resource base to confront a large and wealthy corporate offender, the possible underutilization of sanctions becomes an interesting question.

Part of this chapter is reprinted from "Crime between Organizations: Implications for Victimology," by Diane Vaughan, pp. 77–97 in *White-Collar Crime: Theory and Research*, edited by Gilbert Geis and Ezra Stotland, copyright ©1980 by Sage Publications, Inc., with permission.

A CASE OF COOPTATION?

At the conclusion of the case, the prosecutor's office made statements to the press emphasizing the successful resolution of the largest case of Medicaid provider fraud in the state and the recovery of the funds owed the welfare department.[1] When the outcome was made public, however, this organization was criticized by both primary and peripheral organizations. The members of the network organizations expressed anger in interviews that the Economic Crime Unit had plea-bargained away the case.[2] They felt the evidence they had gathered supported felony charges and a greater number of counts than had been brought against Revco. These other organizations also found that the decisions made by the prosecutor constrained their ability to act on their own against the corporation. Moreover, the peripheral organizations, the attorney general and auditor's offices, both criticized not only the amount of the fine, but also the failure of the welfare department to terminate Revco as a Medicaid provider.[3]

The criticism levied at the Economic Crime Unit concerning the sanctions makes cooptation a relevant issue to consider. Previous research on federal regulatory agencies and their dealings with complex organizations indicates negotiations are frequently influenced by agency cooptation.[4] The model typically associated with regulatory agencies is that of the agency being coopted by a firm which, to avoid the possibility of an enforcement action or reduce its effects, in some way incorporates the members of the agency into its policy-making structure. Agency members become a part of the power structure and take the corporation's view— but the corporation's goal-setting will be influenced as a result. The agency is coopted, the threat to the corporation is diverted, but the policy-making capability of the organization doing the coopting is also influenced.

There is no indication this occurred between Revco and the Economic Crime Unit. Indeed, cooptation is not as likely to be found in a prosecutor's office, which deals with offenders on an ad hoc basis, as it is in an agency that has a continuing responsibility for a particular industry or set of actors.[5] However, this cooptation model may take an unexpected variation which violates the traditional imagery.[6] Rather than the agency posing a threat to the organizations they are designed to control, the reverse may be true: "The regulated pose a threat to the regulators, and the regulators absorb the regulated into their policy-making process of regulation."[7] The business firm's threat derives from the responsibilities of the agency: to regulate, to conclude cases, to prosecute. If firms withhold information and expertise that preclude the agency from accomplishing goals, the stability and existence of the agency may be threatened. Thus, the agency may include the firm in its policy-making process to divert that threat, but the agency's surveillance and enforcement activities will be affected.

There is no evidence that cooptation of this type was a factor in this case. Revco did not impede prosecution by withholding information or expertise from those responsible for social control. In fact, three days after the original prescriptions were seized (two months before plea negotiations began) the corporation promised complete cooperation, identified those in the organization responsible for the false prescriptions, and hired an independent auditing firm to help with the investigation by acting as a liason between Revco and the investigators. Thus, the evidence indicates that neither of the two variations of the cooptation model described above explain the possible underutilization of sanctions in the Revco case. However, a statement of methodological limitations must accompany this conclusion. The full negotiations between Revco and the prosecuting authority were not officially recorded, and no information was available from Revco concerning the determination of sanctions. I reconstructed the negotiations through interviews, memoranda, meeting notes, and documents, all obtained from the network organizations. The final terms were defined in a statement prepared by the prosecution and signed by Revco.

Nonetheless, the antagonism of the other network organizations over the outcome of the plea negotiations was openly expressed in interviews. Had these other organizations felt cooptation had played a role in the outcome, I believe that possibility would have been expressed. Yet no statements were made, nor was there evidence from any of the outside sources (including reporters), that support cooptation as even a partial explanation of the sanction determination. On the one hand, because of methodological limitations, lack of evidence of cooptation does not mean conclusively that it did not occur; on the other hand, perhaps additional research on cooptation would clarify the ways in which its presence or absence vary with the characteristics and environment of the interacting organizations.

However, I did uncover some factors that influenced the sanctioning process and consequently both the material and symbolic sanctions imposed upon Revco.[8] These factors were of a statutory, social, economic, and political nature. They were rooted in the peculiarities of an offense where both victim and offender were large organizations, and they impinged upon the decision-making process of the Economic Crime Unit, the organization responsible for the disposition of the case. As the analysis proceeds, the focus shifts to the exercise of prosecutorial discretion as the key to understanding Revco's sanctioning.

DILEMMAS OF THE PROSECUTION

The successful conclusion of the Revco case was important to the Economic Crime Unit, beyond the organization's legal responsibility to prosecute to the fullest extent of the law. Because it was an election year, bringing Revco severely to task would be a political coup. Moreover, the Economic Crime Unit had been created in 1973 as part of a federally funded nationwide project initiated by the National District Attorneys' Association to combat white-collar crime. When the federal money expired, the support of this unit was assumed by the county. To have the outcome of the case publicly praised would substantiate the unit's continued existence. In addition, the unit was competitive with Economic Crime Units across the country. Effectiveness of each unit was measured and announced to all units monthly and annually by tallies of cases concluded and amount of fines imposed. Resolving the case with maximum penalties would enhance the unit's prestige among similar units. Thus, the prosecution was committed not only to conclude the case, but to conclude it in a way that would bring public acclaim. Not to do so could, indeed, affect the stability and existence of the unit.

Thus, striving for a successful conclusion to the case, the Economic Crime Unit turned to several questions which needed immediate resolution, but for which few precedents existed to guide the prosecution of this multimillion dollar corporate offender:

1. Who should be named in the charge
2. The nature of the charge

3. The number of counts
4. The form of the charge.

However, as these questions one by one were resolved, the sanctioning capabilities of the unit, as well as the other agencies, were circumscribed.

Who Should Be Named in the Charge

The false billings had been submitted in the name of the corporation and the welfare department had reimbursed Revco for them. Yet, the false prescription claims had been the creation of two executives and some temporary clerks hired for the job. According to state trooper interviews, the executives derived no personal gain from the fraud. Instead, the company benefited. Should the executives be charged or the corporation? And if it were the corporation, should the state subsidiary or the parent corporation, located in another state, be charged?

The state criminal code contained statutes which allowed charges to be brought against both the corporation and the two executives. The applicable sections had been created to eliminate the possibility that individuals as well as corporations might use the corporate structure as a shield from liability for corporate acts. The organizational criminal liability statute (Ohio Revised Code, Section 2901.23 [A] [4]) states the circumstances under which an organization may be convicted of an offense. The lack of a suitable penalty, often a stumbling block to organizational criminal liability, was remedied by Ohio Revised Code, Section 2929.31 (organizational penalties). This section provides special penalties (fines) applicable to organizations for every offense, ranging from a fine of not more than one hundred thousand dollars for aggravated murder to not more than one thousand dollars for a minor misdemeanor. Charges could be brought against the two executives through the statute defining personal accountability for organizational conduct (Ohio Revised Code, Section 2901.24). Under this section individuals are subject to the same penalties that they would be had they acted unlawfully in their own behalf.

The question of whether to charge the state subsidiary or the parent corporation was resolved by closer examination of corporate structure. Though billing for prescription claims was handled through corporate offices in Ohio, responsibility for billing in all states rested with the parent corporation in Michigan. More-

charges filed by the prosecutor. From the prosecutor's viewpoint, a bill of information was preferable. The prosecution could avoid increased cost to the county and the problems of proving this case to a grand jury—which would necessitate many complex exhibits, use of computer experts, and rest on evidence which Revco might challenge. Moreover, the decision to proceed by way of information would allow the unit to resolve the case quickly, thus closing off attempts by the attorney general's office to take over the case. Though the unit saw clear advantage to a bill of information, additional gains would result from entering negotiations with this issue apparently unresolved, for Revco also wanted to avoid the publicity and the consequent market impact an indictment would stimulate.

Thus, rather than cooptation, the determination of the sanctions appears to be a normal function of the exercise of prosecutorial discretion. The Economic Crime Unit faced a number of dilemmas. Decisions, ordinarily taken for granted, were without precedent in the Revco case because of the nature of the offense and the offender. Analysis of the prosecution's decision-making process regarding who to name in the charge, the nature of the charge, the number of counts, and the form of the charge indicate some of the stumbling blocks that impeded the sanction determination. Because these decisions were exclusively within the domain of the Economic Crime Unit and the success of the plea negotiations depended upon maintaining secrecy about strategy, the other network organizations were not informed of the strategy or its rationale. Consequently, even before the negotiations began, the prosecutor's office had made decisions about the material sanctions that would offend the other organizations. The charge would be falsification, a misdemeanor; a bill of information would be used to avoid the difficuty of proving the case to a grand jury, lessen the cost, and hasten the proceedings; the case would be plea-bargained for the same reasons and a critical additional one (to gain restitution); and the number of counts would be negotiable to give the unit additional leverage.

At this point, the ability of the pharmacy board to revoke Revco's license and of SUR to terminate the corporation's provider contract already had been blocked. License revocation required a felony charge—an impossibility because the prosecution found that the descriptions of the act in the felony statutes were inaccurate and believed the accompanying penalties were insufficient. The decision about termination of Revco's provider contract hinged not upon statutory considerations, but upon social and economic ones. These factors were touched on in chapter 1, but deserve elaboration here because they raise a broader issue.

Although the termination of Revco's Medicaid provider contract would cost the corporation approximately $2 million annually in Medicaid prescription sales in the state,[13] the potential harm to innocents that imposing this sanction would create was a serious consideration. Indeed, Revco's income from recipient prescriptions would be eliminated, but recipients, some in poor health and without transportation, would be forced to do business with another pharmacy, which would create inconvenience for some, and for others, a hardship. The decision was eventually made by the director of the Department of Public Welfare that Revco would be retained as a provider. This decision was closely guarded, however, even from members of SUR, for it was advantageous to both the Economic Crime Unit and the welfare department that the negotiations be entered into with this issue also apparently unsettled. The termination sanction, though it would not be imposed, would provide the unit with additional bargaining power to be used in obtaining the $521,521.12 in restitution for the welfare department.

ORGANIZATIONS AS SURROGATE VICTIMS

That social and economic considerations were a major influence in the decision not to terminate Revco's provider contract draws attention to an important organizational characteristic that impedes imposition of sanctions. All organizations represent the interests of others.[14] Thus, multiple categories of actors are affected by organizational behavior. For example, the Revco double-billing scheme benefited the corporation by maintaining profit. Simultaneously, the act protected the interests of stockholders by maintaining stock prices and dividends; employees benefited from continued corporate stability; customers benefited from continued competitive prices; the public-at-large benefited from any action that would contribute to a stable economy.

As the organization committing the offense represents multiple categories of actors, so does the victim organization. The Ohio Department of Public Welfare specifically represented the interests of Medicaid recipients. However, as a government agency, the welfare department also represents the public-at-large. Similarly, employees, as organizational members, are relevant. Because these various categories of actors are related to an organization, victimization results in multiple victims. In the Revco case, the welfare department was the direct victim. Financial loss to the department was immediate. However, the loss was dispersed among the other categories of actors which the organization represents. Welfare fraud imposes costs which affect services to recipients, salaries to employees, and taxes on the general public. Though not involved in the interaction with Revco, these other classes of actors become indirect victims.

Illegal behavior between organizations is distinguished from crime between individuals in that victimization is both direct and indirect and multiple victims result. The victimized organization emerges in the role of surrogate victim. Directly victimized, it represents the interests of others which are indirect victims because they also suffer harm. These other victims, however, are seldom visible to the organization committing the offense, and seldom are they aware harm has been done. Hence, they rarely have the ability or the inclination to complain or take action. The organization then becomes a surrogate victim in two ways. First, it is the direct victim, while the other categories of actors which also suffer harm are removed from the illegal act itself. Second, in negotiating with agencies of social control, the surrogate victim acts not only in its own interests, but in behalf of the invisible victims as well. This latter fact may curtail the imposition of sanctions on organizational offenders. In the Revco case, termination of Revco's Medicaid provider contract was not invoked because it would result in hardship and inconvenience for Medicaid recipients. The interests of recipients were in conflict with the interests of the public-at-large to control organizational illegality by imposition of sanctions. Not wishing to victimize its own clients, welfare chose not to impose this sanction on Revco.

Use of other sanctions, both material and symbolic, were similarly curtailed because of concern for the interests of other categories of actors. The Economic Crime Unit was a commonweal organization representing the interests of the public-at-large, which included public investors in the stock market. Throughout the case, the size of the corporation and amount and scope of the fraud had attracted national attention. Financial analysts from all over the country repeatedly called the prosecutor's office for information which could be used to advise existing and potential stockholders. The prosecution's concern for impact on the market resulted in tight control of information, and encouraged decisions that led to a swift and quiet resolution. Concern for stock market investors was balanced against the interests of the public-at-large in control of organizational illegality. The official role of this organization required that the divergent interests of various segments of the public be taken into account. The interests of all these categories of actors could not be served simultaneously. The prosecution proceeded in ways that minimized financial impact on stockholders.

Revco, however, received this same benefit. The process of sanctioning by a legal authority is broader than the final outcome of a case, e.g., the $50,000 fine and restitution required of Revco. The investigation itself has the potential to initiate symbolic sanctions, for related publicity can stir public reaction, with possible economic repercussions for the offending organization through the stock market.[15] However, because of the unwillingness of both the prosecution and welfare department to impose sanctions which could have harmed categories of actors these organizations perceived as innocents, and because of the other burdens of the prosecution had the case gone to trial, the potential sanctions available in the Revco case were not used to the fullest. The need for organizations to balance the interests of others does not end with Revco, the welfare department, or the prosecuting authority, however. The Ohio State Highway Patrol and the Ohio State Board of Pharmacy, too, were charged with protecting the interests of the public-at-large. Each had a vested interest in the final sanctions imposed. The compromises made by the prosecuting authority on behalf of investors were in conflict with the interests represented by these other organizations. Though the prosecuting authority also represented the public-at-large, the official role of this organization required the divergent interests of various segments of the public to be taken into account.

There are several implications here concerning offenses committed by organizations against other organizations. First, when an organization is victimized, there are multiple victims. The organization, the direct victim, is surrogate for its beneficiaries, the indirect victims. As these other categories of actors are incapable of acting in their own behalf, the organization, as surrogate victim, assumes this function. Second, the offender and the victim organizations may be dealt with by one or more social control organizations. Though the social control function may benefit by an increase in potential sanctions, the involvement of multiple organizations means additional interests must be balanced. The interests of all these categories of actors can seldom be served simultaneously. Because both material and symbolic sanctions against the offender have the potential to create additional classes of victims, some interests may be compromised in behalf of others. Thus, the potential impact of the sanctions may be mitigated.

IMPACT OF INVESTIGATION AND FORMAL SANCTIONS ON REVCO

At the close of the investigation, Revco was sentenced according to the negotiated plea agreement. The corporation was ordered to make restitution of $521,521.12 to the Ohio Department of Public Welfare and to pay a $50,000 fine. Examination of the impact of these sanctions, as well as the investigation, is limited because Revco's corporate records of personnel turnover, short-run and long-run sales patterns, transactions with drug manufacturers and distributors, auditing costs, legal fees, and other internal organizational indicators were unavailable.

Nevertheless, impact was measurable through publicly available information.[16] First, the impact of restitution and fine, totaling $571,521.12, was compared to the approximately $650 million in total sales for the company's then most recent fiscal year ending 28 May 1977.[17] The sanctions imposed amounted to less than .001 percent of gross. Oberg indicated "the settlement resulted in a .03 write-off to fourth quarter earnings per share in the year ended May 31, 1977. Since this amount was not material in nature, the company did not footnote it separately in either its 1977 annual report or 10-K filed for that period."[18]

Then, on the basis of a financial comparison conducted for the years 1971 through 1978, three drug retailers similar to Revco were selected.[19] Statistics supported the homogeneity of the industry during this period.[20] Stock price movement, earnings, and price/earnings ratios of Revco were compared to those of the other three drug retailers from 1 January 1977 through June 1978. This analysis was balanced against market activity for the drug industry over an extended period. Prior to the Medicaid fraud investigation and settlement, earnings and stock price movements of the four companies were correlated closely.[21] Revco's stock price and price/earnings ratios, when examined in relation to newspaper publicity about the case, however, clearly differed from the activity of the other three drug retailers during the period of the investigation.[22]

The first newspaper announcement of the investigation on 29 April 1977 precipitated the divergent pattern for Revco. Volume expanded sharply and the stock's price declined.[23] Similar fluctuations occurred with subsequent publicity. Revco's stock price and price/earnings ratio ranges varied, but remained depressed throughout the investigation. These patterns did not occur for the comparison companies. Oberg reports, "After the July 28, 1977 announcement of the settlement, the stock's price began to show slight upward movement. This trend continued as the company announced an earnings increase of 23% for the year ending in May of 1977 and a sales advance of 19%."[24] The first six months of 1978 indicated Revco's activity no longer deviated from patterns of market activity displayed by the comparison companies, but again paralleled them. Oberg concludes:

> While there was a very sharp, downward reaction of the price and price/earnings ratio of Revco's stock, once the litigation was settled and good earnings gains were reported the price of the stock rebounded. By early in 1978 the investment community had essentially "forgotten" the incident and the shares had regained a favorable investment status. As Stuart Robbins of Mitchell Hutchins suggested in his report of August 21, 1977, the monetary cost to the company was small and the independent audit reaffirmed the excellent quality of management and good internal controls. So from a financial analytical point of view the problem was solved. The company emerged intact and no future disruptions could be anticipated. Focus could again be placed on earnings and sales trends. Sales remained strong through 1977 and 1978, which seems to indicate that the settlement and admitted wrongdoing had not tarnished Revco's image as a price leader or caused a consumer reaction of boycotting the store.[25]

51

A stockholder report published by Revco at the close of the third quarter, 4 February 1978, compares the firm's activities with a similar report issued in February 1977, the quarter before the investigation became public:

> Net sales increased 21 percent, earnings before tax increased 18 percent and net earnings were up 21 percent from the comparable period a year ago.

> Net sales were $195 million compared with $161.7 million. Earnings before taxes were $15.2 million vs. 12.9 million. Net earnings were $7.7 million or $.58 per common share compared with $6.3 million or $.48 per common share a year ago.

> The most recent dividend, which was paid March 16 to shareholders of record on March 2, 1978, more than doubled the payment rate of a year ago and was the second increase in Revco's current fiscal year. This new March dividend was paid at the rate of 13 cents per common share, up 30 percent from the 10 cents per share paid last December.

> We lead our industry in numbers of outlets, and cemented this leadership in February with the dedication of our 1,000th store. Revco operates in 23 states and is adding new retail outlets at the rate of one every four days with 1,014 in operation today.[26]

There are certain boundaries to the conclusions to be drawn concerning the impact of the investigation and settlement on Revco. I had no opportunity to control for factors within the organization that may have contributed to the rise and fall of selected indicators during the period in question; for example, changes in policy, marketing practices, or personnel. However, four observations can be made with confidence: (1) the amount of the settlement was almost negligible compared to the total sales of the company; (2) market activity deviated in downward trends from patterns exhibited by comparable drug retailers during the investigation; (3) after the settlement, Revco's stock prices and price/earnings ratios again paralleled the behavior of competitors; and (4) in the subsequent twelve-month period, Revco set record highs in sales, earnings, and dividends.

The settlement was the largest fine and greatest amount of restitution ever recorded in the state. Nonetheless, the available indicators reflect that the investigation had a short-run negative impact on Revco's well-being, from which the corporation quickly recovered. A perhaps greater effect of the investigation and settlement stemmed from the political reaction to the case, which resulted in permanent change in the structure and function of the social control network, as noted in chapter 2. One might say that Revco emerged from the investigation relatively unchanged and intact, but the network did not. However, in addition to the impact of the sanctions and the processes that shaped the decision making, another important finding is the potential of the network to regulate the behavior of the corporation in this case.

Recall that the backlog of rejected claims that caused corporate officials to falsify prescriptions in the first place originated because Revco had failed to update their own internal edit system, programmed to identify errors in claims before they were transmitted to the welfare department for reimbursement. Had Revco's system been working properly, welfare officials alleged, the backlog of rejected claims could have been avoided and reimbursement would not have been delayed. The welfare department made revision of Revco's computer claims submission apparatus a condition of resumption of reimbursement for current claims. Members of the computer systems teams of both Revco and the welfare department worked together to eliminate system problems. Revco's internal edit system was updated and new programs were installed. Not only that, but claims submitted by Revco were subject to new computer screening devices and frequent manual review by the department for a year after the case was closed. At last report, Revco's rejection rates were within the average for providers of comparable size and services. Thus, though the official sanctions appeared to have no long-term effect on the corporation, the origin of the problem was corrected, and monitoring equipment was in place to guard against a reoccurrence. The investigation led to a remedy for the specific problem that generated the unlawful behavior and close surveillance was initiated as a preventive mechanism.

4

Toward Understanding Unlawful Organizational Behavior

A case study is exactly that: a study of a single case. Yet to isolate the case from the social structure in which it occurs is to attempt to study it in a vacuum. Though empirical substantiation of the total structural context in which a particular event is embedded is out of the question, the researcher has a responsibility to be cognizant of this broader context and to fit the case within it to whatever extent possible. The Revco case occurred within a specific social structure that has been carved out of the larger one for research purposes. The specific social structure is comprised of the organizations that interacted in the event: as offender, as victim, and as agents of social control. It also occurred within the social structure of American society, in which unlawful organizational behavior has a long history and vast resources are directed toward its control. Thus, while impossible to generalize from any case study, it is important to frame the Revco investigation against this larger backdrop, to examine and consider this broader setting, in order to better understand unlawful organizational behavior and efforts at social control.[1]

The setting is one in which organizational misconduct is systematically produced by the social structure. By social structure, I mean (1) the stable characteristics in American society that form the environment in which organizations conduct their business activities: sets of social relations, laws, norms, groups, institutions; and (2) the stable characteristics of organizations themselves: internal structure, processes, and the nature of transactions. These factors produce tensions for organizations to attain goals

Part of this chapter is reprinted with permission from Diane Vaughan, "Toward Understanding Unlawful Organizational Behavior," *Michigan Law Review*, June 1982.

unlawfully. Although not all organizations experiencing these tensions will respond with misconduct, the pages that follow seek to open lines of inquiry by presenting the relationship between these structural factors and unlawful behavior as a general model. While applicable to the unlawful behavior of organizations other than those engaged in private enterprise, this explication focuses on profit-seeking complex organizations in the legitimate economic order because these organizations present the strongest example.

THE STRUCTURAL IMPETUS

The idea that the social structure generates the motivation for individuals to engage in deviance was suggested by Merton.[2] The concepts central to his thesis are competition, economic success as a culturally approved goal, and erosion of norms supporting legitimate procedures for achieving it. More specifically, Merton suggests that the interplay between the cultural structure and the social structure play a critical role in the production of deviance. He focuses on two elements of the cultural structure: (1) culturally defined goals (ends) that are held out and accepted as legitimate objectives for all members of a society, and (2) norms that specify the allowable procedures (means) for attaining these objectives. When the achievement of the desired goals receives strong cultural emphasis, while much less emphasis is placed on the norms regulating the means, these norms will tend to lose their power to regulate behavior. A state of anomie (normlessness) develops. Given the culturally induced motivation to succeed and the decreased effectiveness of norms, "innovation," or the pursuit of desired goals by expedient but socially proscribed means, may be the response.[3]

Having suggested innovation as a mode of adaptation, Merton seeks to uncover the structural conditions which precipitate this form of deviance. Though he discusses at some length the deviant business practices of the elite, citing anecdotes from Dickens and data from Sutherland, he assumes, apparently on the basis of official crime statistics and research relating crime to poverty, that the social structure exerts greater pressures toward deviation on the lower class.[4] Merton concludes that among the lower class the cultural emphasis on success has taken hold, but socially structured access to conventional and legitimate means for be-

While examining the potential consequences of unequal avenues to the competition (blocked access to legitimate means), Merton ignores the possible outcomes for those who do compete. His focus on blocked access to legitimate means presents only a part of the explanation. His position is that the social structure allows some to compete for goals and excludes others. Those competing follow institutionally prescribed norms and those excluded do not.[13] He implicitly assumes equal access to goals. Not all who compete, however, can win. Not only are the legitimate avenues to pursue culturally approved goals differentially distributed, but the desired resources which represent the goals are themselves in short supply. The result is competition for both means and ends.[14] The structural availability of both means and ends can be limited, moreover, not only by insufficient supply, but also by the inability or unwillingness to obtain a commodity at a given price. Thus, some scarcity can always exist. And when a competitor is threatened with possible loss in that legitimate competition due to scarcity of means or ends, innovation may result.

Profit-seeking organizations must compete to secure the strategic resources they need.[15] They compete not only for economic goals, but also for the resources that are the means to economic ends: personnel recruitment, product development, land acquisition, advertising space, sales territory. An organization's ability to obtain requisite resources may be constrained by the source, nature, and abundance of the resource, by the behavior of other organizations in the environment in the roles of consumers, suppliers, competitors, and controllers, by individuals in the role of consumers, and by the resources already possessed by the organization and pre-existing demands on those resources.[16] As a result, attainment of economic goals may be obstructed in two ways: (1) legitimate means are blocked, hence the organization is excluded from the competition (e.g., market entry is prohibited by controllers; resources are unavailable to devote to product development);[17] and (2) an organization might gain entry to the competition, but despite conformity to socially prescribed mechanisms, be unable to attain its economic goals because supplies of the resources that represent the goals (e.g., government contracts; customers for a particular product) are limited. Because profit-seeking organizations strive not only for goals, but also for the means to those goals, both can be reconceptualized as resources for which organizations must compete. And when the scarcity of strategic resources threatens an organization with possible loss in legitimate competition, unlawful conduct may result.[18]

The likelihood that an organization will act unlawfully is not, of course, determined solely by competition for strategic resources. The effect of goal variability on the competition must also be considered. All organizations must maximize returns over costs to survive, but the more general goal of economic success will be reflected in differential standards in particular organizations. Economic success is relative, and an organization's criteria for success are shaped by both financial conditions and by the other organizations with which it must compete. Standards for success reflect position in the organizational stratification system, and may take three forms:[19]

1. A shift in economic and social position; higher status competitors.
2. A shift in economic position; higher status among same competitors.
3. Maintenance of existing economic and social position.

For organizations already among the elite, an upward shift in social position may not be possible, although higher status within the same membership group may be. Organizations not among the elite may, at varying times, be concerned with all three standards for success. And all organizations, regardless of rank, must seek to maintain their existing economic and social position. To fail to maintain that position is to succumb to downward mobility. Consequently, scarcity, combined with the differential standards for economic success, raises the possibility of blocked access to resources *regardless of an organization's size, wealth, age, experience, or previous record.*

Economic goals may vary in a second important way. Competitive pressures and the cultural emphasis on economic success typically lead organizations to establish new goals once one is achieved.[20] A "maximum" profit, in the literal sense, becomes an infinitely receding possibility under these circumstances. Motivational pressures continue to operate, reinforcing the continued pursuit of success. Should a goal be attained, a new one is set, continually recreating the possibility of blocked access to resources and the consequent tensions to attain them by innovative but socially proscribed means.

Innovation, according to Merton, is likely to be chosen as a survival strategy when support diminishes for legitimate procedures for reaching desired goals. The erosion of normative support for legitimate conduct among organizations has been noted in the stratification system of societies that become modernized.[21] The importance of family lineage as the basis of rank declines, while the ranking of organizations relative to one another becomes increasingly important. Organizational membership becomes an indicator of individual prestige. In this way, individuals' mobility becomes linked to improving the position of their organization relative to other organizations. In a society that is not experiencing major structural reorganization, the norms governing the competition for rank among organizations usually obtain consensus. When modernization is underway, however, the established stratification principles are inappropriate. The units to be ranked are organizations, not families, and the ranking process is further complicated by the rapid multiplication of organizations. Consensus is absent on the ranks of organizations and how the ranks may legitimately be improved.

New organizations, moreover, tend to be led by new leaders, who did not previously occupy elite positions. Because of youth and a rapid rise to wealth and prominence, these new leaders tend to be "less committed to the norms of the system of stratification among organizations."[22] Unsocialized by the old elite, their behavior is guided by the principle that new organizations only rise rapidly if they have some disrespect for traditional standards.[23] Thus, in a period of rapid structural differentiation,

> the question is the degree of commitment to norms governing the interorganizational distribution of wealth, power, and prestige according to accepted norms. There is no acceptable sense in which one can say that the organizational leaders in an anomic situation engage in 'deviant behavior'. *What is very generally at stake is the definition of what is deviant* [emphasis added].[24]

Under these circumstances, the means of organizational competition become unlimited.

These characteristics attributed to modernizing societies appear to continue in highly modernized societies. Because some organizations cease to exist and others are constantly being created, the ranking of organizations remains in flux. Organizational membership continues to be a key element defining individual prestige. Perhaps most important, the definition of deviance remains ambiguous, creating the possibility of a chronic state of anomie for all organizations, *regardless of rank in the stratification system.* In the business world, the lines between a good business deal and illegality often do become blurred.[25] Merton notes, "On the top economic levels, the pressure toward innovation not infrequently erases the distinction between business-like strivings this side of the mores and sharp practices beyond the mores."[26]

Successful achievement of organizational goals through unlawful conduct tends to reinforce the occurrence of this behavior, so that what the society defines as illegal may come to be defined in the organization as normative. Choice is not simply an output of structure, but a strategic input for the system as a whole. The successful become models for others in their environment who, initially less vulnerable and alienated, now no longer keep to the rules that they once regarded as legitimate.[27] Decisions to use illegitimate methods to achieve desired goals thus feed back into the social structure, effectively maintaining the pattern "unless counteracting mechanisms of social control are called into play."[28]

Because organizations succeed in having their special values advanced and protected through the enactment of legal norms, these "countervailing mechanisms" operate at less than maximum effectiveness. This is true because administrative rules and regulations and criminal and civil statutes that are directed at organizational behavior do not revolve around sacred values—in fact, in many cases represent no values of individuals—but instead result from compromises reached between regulatory agencies or legislatures and the firms they regulate.[29] Unlawful behavior thus receives additional structural support, which aids in maintaining the pattern. The success of some organizations at attaining their goals unlawfully encourages others to follow the same path to success.[30] The absence of normative support for legitimate conduct is replaced by normative support for the illegitimate but expedient. Carried to the extreme, norm erosion might become so extensive within an organization or a subunit of an organization that unlawful conduct occurs regardless of resource scarcity. Behavior that, if viewed by society, would be considered unlawful may come to be considered acceptable business practice and nondeviant within the organization.

As normative support for legitimate procedures erodes, organizations motivated by the cultural emphasis on economic success and the need to survive, and unable to attain resources legitimately, may instead resort to technically expedient but unlawful behavior. Anticompetitive actions like price-fixing and discriminatory price-cutting, theft of trade secrets, false advertising, and bribery and payoffs to ensure market share could thus be described as the victimization of one organization by another to obtain resources that facilitate upward mobility in the organizational stratification system.[31] Similarly, organizations seeking either a change in economic position that will bring higher status among similarly situated organizations, or merely to maintain their economic position may also act unlawfully under these circumstances.[32]

SUMMARY AND IMPLICATIONS

Economic success, competition for scarce resources, and norm erosion provide some insight into how unlawful organizational behavior may be systematically produced by the social structure. Organizations must pursue economic success in order to survive. However, attainment of this general goal can be blocked in two ways: (1) legitimate means are blocked, thus the organization cannot enter the competition; and (2) legitimate means are available, but once in the competition, the organization may not succeed because the resources that represent the goals are limited. Thus, both means and ends, whatever their material referent, are resources that by their scarcity may inhibit goal attainment for organizations, regardless of position in the stratification system. In addition, competitive necessities and the cultural emphasis on success exert pressure to achieve new ends, converting any achievement into simply another rung on the long ladder of success. The competitor, then, is subject to social pressures to remain in the competition, raising again the possibility of blocked access to resources. Because the achievement of economic success receives strong cultural emphasis (and is, in fact, a necessity for organizational survival) while much less emphasis is placed on the norms regulating the means to success, the norms have tended to lose the power to regulate behavior. Consequently, organizations finding resources structurally unavailable may seek economic success by unlawful methods.

To what types of organizations might these concepts apply? As presented, they are directed toward understanding the unlawful behavior of profit-seeking complex organizations in the legitimate economic order. I suggested earlier, however, that applicability is not restricted to profit-seeking business organizations. A brief discussion at this point is worthwhile to indicate the logic behind my original statement and how other organizations may or may not be included. Three types of complex organizations come to mind: (1) organizations designed to fail, (2) nonprofit organizations, and (3) organizations operating in the illegitmate economic order: organized crime.

Organizations Designed to Fail

Not all organizations seek profits. Some, in fact, were designed to accumulate losses, rather than profits. The individual owner or owners receive benefits, while the organization is the center of transactions and loss.[33] These organizations obviously do not fit a motivational scheme based on competition to acquire resources in order to survive.

Non-Profit Organizations

Some organizations are designed to seek neither profits nor losses: for example, churches, voluntary associations, government, state-supported universities, community self-help organizations. Regardless of their diverse goals, they must acquire resources. In the acquisition of resources, as well as in other organizational activities, nonprofit organizations do engage in economic activity encompassing the production, exchange, distribution, and consumption of goods and services. While necessary resources and other activities may not themselves be viewed as profits or mechanisms for obtaining profits, these organizations must maximize returns in order to exist.

Organizations Operating in the Illegitimate Economic Order

The organized crime enterprise engages in business activities which extend into both the legitimate and illegitimate economic

63

orders. In both instances, organizational survival depends upon the ability to maximize returns. Though the means used to seek profits may be illegitimate, these organizations certainly are engaged in competition for economic success. The case of organized crime raises an interesting point for speculation. While the origins of organized crime may be attributed in part to blocked access to legitimate means,[34] the continued use of unlawful behavior may call for a different explanation. One principle behind organized crime is that illegitimate means become institutionalized. Therefore, some organizations within the organized crime enterprise may never find legitimate means blocked because once illegitimate means are institutionalized, legitimate means are abandoned. Unlawful conduct may then be perpetuated by the development of normative solidarity supporting the use of illegitimate methods to attain goals—regardless of resource scarcity.[35]

To what types of behaviors might these concepts apply? They fit the activities of organizations that violate the law in pursuit of culturally approved goals, broadly defined as economic success. This criterion excludes behavior that is not directed toward maximizing returns, such as violations that occur through mistake. A law or regulation may be violated because it is misunderstood, or because its existence is unknown. Other violations may occur, such as sex discrimination in hiring, for which the linkage between the violation and profit-making remains a matter of empirical inquiry. Consider also violations that occur through negligence. Because business firms do take risks in the name of profit, negligence may occur as a result of profit-seeking activity. If it can be determined that a firm was negligent because resources were allocated to maximize profits at the expense of proper attention to some task, the concepts would be relevant to the organization's behavior. In this and similar situations, the inability to make the necessary empirical determinations may be a serious impediment. In addition, organizations may engage in unlawful behavior which does not appear to require research to determine the lack of conceptual fit: for example, organizations that engage in conspiracy in order to overthrow government, or religious organizations that deprive members of liberty or life.[36] Nevertheless, current opinion on the link between objectives, regardless of diversity, and the need for organizations to maximize returns for continued existence suggests that the model developed here is generally valid.[37]

While no explanation has yet been found which encompasses all forms of organizational misconduct, the structural factors suggested on these pages do appear to apply to many instances of unlawful organizational behavior.[38] Admittedly, no single paradigm can serve as a tool for investigating the entire range of intriguing questions concerning organizational misconduct. A social-psychological explanation, for example, may provide acceptable answers to some questions.[39] Nonetheless, thinking about organizations in terms of structural pressures to engage in unlawful behavior explains a good deal of what is known and surmised about the phenomenon in question. The extent to which the fit is true, however, must be verified by empirical test.

Admittedly, acknowledging that means and ends are not only variable, but in many instances indistinguishable except under close examination in the specific situation, makes translation of these concepts into testable general hypotheses difficult. Nonetheless, the sociologist's task is not to come up with explanations that are easy to test. The task is to formulate explanations that make sense. If what makes sense is difficult to test, then rather than rejecting it, the underlying theoretical question should become the subject of research and interpretation.[40] Despite this lack of closure, or perhaps because of it, these concepts appear to have considerable heuristic value for research. Reconceptualizing means and ends as resources for which organizations must compete expands the possibility for measurement at the structural level. Regardless of teleological questions which may cloud the distinction between means and ends, the controversy can be circumvented in the case of organizations by measuring resource scarcity and its relationship to organizational behavior. Whereas in the past "availability of legitimate means" often has been examined in terms of individual attitudes toward job opportunities,[41] availability can be operationally defined in structural terms as, for example, the number of organizations competing for a cable television franchise in a given territory, or under airline regulation, the number of organizations competing for a license giving them the right to serve city pairs.

Of similar research interest is the question of norm erosion. Too often the erosion of normative support for lawful conduct is assumed simply on the basis of the observed frequency of violations. We need to ask other questions. Does existence or erosion of normative support vary by industry, technology, or size of firm? By the desired resources? By the availability of alternatives? At what point can normative support for use of legitimate methods to obtain scarce resources be said to be eroded? Or, perhaps the fundamental research agenda should be to determine to what extent it is lack of norms, norm erosion, or the conflict between government norms and internally generated norms that contribute to organizational misconduct. Historical studies of the relationship between organizational misconduct and these structural factors also are needed.

A most puzzling question, unresolved in research to date and promising future difficulty, evolves from the suggestion that all organizations, regardless of rank in the stratification system, may be subject to structural strain. Not all organizations experiencing these tensions resort to illegal behavior, however.[42] Why do some engage in unlawful conduct while others do not? This question is explored in the next two chapters.

5

Opportunities for Unlawful Organizational Behavior

While the social structure may produce tensions for organizations to seek scarce resources by illegal methods, unlawful behavior cannot be explained by these structural tensions alone. Opportunities must be available to obtain resources unlawfully.[1] Indeed, opportunities to attain resources unlawfully but through legitimate mechanisms are inherent in all complex organizations operating in the legitimate economic order because of the nature of organizational processes, structure, and transactions. Created for the purpose of conducting legitimate business activity, these factors may also promote unlawful behavior by (1) providing normative support for illegality, (2) providing mechanisms for carrying out illegal acts, and (3) minimizing the risk of detection and sanctioning. As a consequence, organizations may respond to blocked access to desired resources by turning to the opportunities within their own boundaries to attain them unlawfully.

Organizational characteristics have frequently been hypothesized to encourage unlawful organizational conduct.[2] The factors examined include firm longevity, product diversification, financial performance, geographic expansion, market power, and size.[3] What these characteristics have in common is that they are researchable—this information is publicly available, through corporate financial statements and mandatory agency filing requirements. But other organizational characteristics—for example, processes and structure that are internal and, therefore, more elusive for research purposes—play an important role in

Parts of this chapter are reprinted from Diane Vaughan, "Toward Understanding Unlawful Organizational Behavior," *Michigan Law Review*, June 1982, and from "Transaction Systems and Unlawful Organizational Behavior," *Social Problems* 29, no. 5 (1982): 373–379. Permission granted from the Society for the Study of Social Problems.

the unlawful conduct of business firms that may complicate the findings concerning those factors that have been studied. Organizational size, for example, has been the most frequently investigated factor thought to be related to violations that are committed by one organization against another.[4] The larger the organization, it has been hypothesized, the more frequent the violations. The evidence, however, has been contradictory. Perhaps a more satisfactory hypothesis is that it is not simply size per se that facilitates the unlawful conduct of organizations, but the complexity of the internal processes and structure that accompany increased size that explain the behavior.[5]

This chapter examines how structure, processes, and transaction systems create opportunities for organizations to act as offenders. Before turning to this topic, I want to make three points: first, these same factors create an arena where individuals may readily engage in misconduct that is in their own interest, separate and distinct from the interests of the organization. Second, the opportunities inherent in business firms not only create the potential for an organization to engage in unlawful conduct, but also promote the possibility that an organization will be victimized—by other organizations as well as by its own members. Finally, although these same opportunities exist in general form for all organizations, the conditions and combinations of factors that do or do not result in unlawful behavior cannot yet be unraveled. They cannot, therefore, be discussed in the language of causality, but rather in terms of factors that facilitate, generate, encourage, or present opportunities to attain resources through unlawful conduct.

ORGANIZATIONAL PROCESSES

Processes are the dynamics of organizational life that affect individual members. While introducing the notion of organizations as actors is legitimate and effectively accounts for certain actions, organizations must rely on individuals to act as their agents. To describe properly the behavior—lawful or unlawful— of organizations, therefore, we need an explanation that goes beyond the goals and actions of the organization to the nexus of the goals and actions of the organization and the goals and actions of its members.[6] This necessity draws attention to the internal processes of organizations and to the normative environment that results.

It is common knowledge that organizations selectively recruit new members who in many ways match those already there. But individuals come to business firms influenced by their affiliations with other organizations: families, churches, clubs, schools, trade unions, and previous employers. Because business firms depend on their members to attain goals, they must ensure that members' skills, motivations, and values are consistent with the organization's needs. To the extent that members subscribe to, support, and are willing and able to pursue organizational interests, the firm's chances for survival are enhanced.

The existence of these important characteristics of members is, not surprisingly, rarely left to chance. As Selznick notes, "the more esoteric the activities of the organization, the less it can rely on the general education provided by the community, and the greater the need for internal orientation."[7] Most organizations, therefore, subject new recruits to education and training. Skills are taught, sharpened, and adjusted to meet organizational needs through both formal and informal mechanisms: training classes, apprenticeships, peer groups, and mentoring. Integral to the mechanisms operating to develop these skills are systematic socialization processes that attune members ideologically to the organization's goals.

Educational and training programs are supplemented, and perhaps eventually superseded, by an internal reward system incorporating both remuneration and prestige. The rewards are often formal, tangible, and obvious to other employees and even outsiders: promotion, bonuses, salary increases, profit-sharing, parking privileges, expense accounts, gold watches, company cars, employee-of-the-month awards, titles, attractive offices, and assistants. In other cases, the rewards are informal and not so obvious, but are powerful incentives, especially in the upper echelon, because of their long-term impact on a career. Use of first names, inclusion in after-hours get-togethers with management officials, or an invitation to play golf with the boss reward the employee with admission to the informal organization of the firm's elite. Behavior inconsistent with organizational goals typically leads to negative sanctions. These, too, can be formal (loss of parking privileges, loss of an assistant, or a shift to a deadend position) or informal (exclusion from the boss's golf outing). The ultimate sanction, of course, is a requested resignation or firing. Large organizations, moreover, tend increasingly to absorb members, while at the same time insulating them from the outside world.[8] Skills and language for a particular task may be so specialized that an employee cannot find similar work in other organizations. Members with no alternative skills are tied to the firm by financial dependence. Accumulated retirement benefits and delayed remuneration also encourage long-term commitments to organizations. Profit-sharing not only encourages long-term commitments, but gives the individual a stake in the system. The luster of future financial rewards binds members to the organization like a pair of golden handcuffs securing their continued affiliation with the firm. And recreational activities, committee work, company cafeterias and corporate dining rooms, long hours, special projects and frequent transfers separate an organizaton's members from the outside community and foster a dependence upon the organization that is social, as well as financial.

In these and other ways, the needs of the individual member eventually become linked to the organization's success. Because a primary criterion of individuals' status in highly modernized societies is the social status of the organizations to which they belong,[9] the individual identifies with the organization and the organization's goals. The organization's ability to attain desired resources affects the ability of members to be upwardly mobile, to improve their economic position while remaining in the same social class, or simply to preserve their existing position. Because the interests of members and organizations coincide, employees may engage in unlawful behavior in the organization's behalf, using the skills, knowledge, and resources associated with their position do so.

Organizational processes, then, create an internal moral and intellectual world in which the individual identifies with the organization and the organization's goals. The survival of the one becomes linked to the survival of the other, and a normative environment evolves that, given difficulty in attaining scarce resources, encourages illegal behavior to attain them. But some finer distinctions must be made. Not all agents of an organization will act illegally in the organization's behalf. The nature of the response—lawful or unlawful behavior—will be shaped by structural factors both internal and external to the organization. While organizations may experience structural tensions to violate legal norms, variation in subunit membership, position in the information system, and rewards and punishments may undermine the organization's ability to unify the goals and actions of its members with its own goals and actions, producing either deviance or conformity to legal norms.[10]

Subunit Membership

Tensions to attain resources unlawfully affect the various parts of the organization differentially. The subunits with skills and resources most relevant to profit-seeking goals are most likely to be affected.[11] Because of the many and changing goals of organizations, the subunits affected may vary over time, and some may never experience such tensions. Members of subunits not subject to these tensions will not be motivated to engage in illegal behavior in the organization's behalf.

Position in the Information System

Though working in a subunit that is experiencing tensions that could precipitate misconduct, members without information about necessary resources and difficulties in attaining them will not be motivated to act illegally in the organization's behalf. For unlawful behavior to occur, the member's position must provide access to information regarding the organization's goals as they relate to the activities of the subunit in which the member is employed. The position, moreover, must entail some responsibility for goal attainment. Finally, the position must provide skills and resources that allow the individual to resolve the organization's difficulties.

Rewards and Punishments

Even if subunit membership and position in the information system create tensions to engage in unlawful behavior in the organization's behalf, members thus situated may not do so. Norms and values learned through association with other organizations (both formal and informal) may compete with and contradict those learned while in the firm.[12] Should the norms be contradictory, members will make choices in accordance with the rewards and punishments accompanying the various alternatives.[13] Members will weigh the possibility of gaining rewards against the possibility of incurring punishment, and thus, cost. Lemert notes, "Costs are important variables in analysis because changes in costs of means can modify the order of choices, even though the 'ideal' value order of the individual remains constant."[14]

As the rewards and punishments accompanying the alternatives vary, the patterns of individual choice will vary. Should the firm's rewards for gaining the desired resources outweigh the perceived costs of pursuing them unlawfully, members may commit violations on behalf of the organization despite competing norms. Again, position in the information system is relevant, for information flows affect the probability that rewards and punishments will be meted out—both internal and external to the organization.[15] The significance of the organization's rewards and punishments, moreover, will vary as the individual's dependence upon the firm varies. Alternative skills, alternative sources of income, and alternative validating social roles reduce financial and social dependence on the firm.[16] Consequently, external reward and punishments may reduce the organization's ability to mobilize individual efforts in its behalf, despite processes that produce a normative environment supporting unlawful conduct.

Although all organizations create normative environments that join the goals and actions of members to those of the firm, to assert that organizational processes uniformly produce a fertile atmosphere for illegality obscures the complexity that exists. The degree to which an organization experiences pressures to act unlawfully varies not only by subunit, but within subunits, and over time. The ability and willingness of members to act illegally in the organization's behalf depend on the subunit in which they work, their position in the information system, and the weighing of rewards and punishments. These factors may not only generate lawful conduct in the face of organizational pressures to violate, but may generate unlawful conduct despite a normative environment that supports compliance with legal norms. It is important to recognize, therefore, that the normative environment generated by organizational processes will have a variable relationship to unlawful conduct, and that the problem of measurement remains a powerful obstacle to a complete understanding of the relationship between internal environment and behavior.

ORGANIZATIONAL STRUCTURE

The structure of complex organizations creates opportunities by (1) providing many settings where unlawful behavior might occur, and (2) isolating those settings and masking organizational behavior, thus reducing the risk of detection and sanctioning. Size and the complexity that frequently accompanies size provide many locations in which unlawful behavior might take place. As organizations grow larger, specialized subunits result, each providing opportunities to engage in unlawful behavior on the organization's behalf. Not only are organizations internally diversified in ways that multiply the possible settings for illegality, but many organizations are geographically dispersed, with locations throughout the United States and the world, greatly expanding the number of locations in which unlawful behavior might occur.

These specialized subunits compete for resources with other organizations and with each other.[17] The need for a subunit to outperform other organizations, other units within the same organization, or even its own previous record to secure resources from the parent organization may generate illegality, such as falsification of records, or theft of trade secrets. Subunits have concerns about their own survival that may or may not coincide with the interests of the larger organization, and if given an opportunity to exercise discretion, lower-level managers will tend to act not to maximize the firm's welfare, but rather to enhance the interests of their own unit or division.[18] In a recent book on the internal workings of General Motors, for example, the corporation's continual competition with the Ford Motor Company bears striking similarities to the description of the rivalry between two divisions of General Motors, Chevrolet and Pontiac, as well as to the adversarial relationship between the divisions of the company and their respective dealers.[19]

Specialization not only generates opportunities for unlawful behavior by increasing the locations where it might occur, but also obscures organizational behavior, lawful and unlawful. Task segregation cloaks activities. No one individual or group can command all the knowledge pertaining to particular operations, materials, or technology.[20] This serves a protective function for the organization, increasing its ability to survive despite information leakage or personnel turnover.[21] The secrecy generated by task segregation, however, also enhances the opportunity for misconduct. Specialization leads to problems of coordination and control. Consequently, organizations develop rules and procedures to handle the various internal contingencies the organization faces by specifying how, when, and by whom tasks are to be performed.[22] The rules and procedures are expressed in a language common to all subunits of an organization, symbolically integrating the various parts. They seek not only to control and coordinate activities, but also to facilitate the systematic exchange of information that is necessary for decision making.

Though directed toward integrating the separate parts of the organization, the potential for rules and procedures to achieve internal coordination and control varies considerably. Progressive loss of control over subunits seems to be a natural consequence of organizational growth. Structure interferes with the efforts of those at the top to "know" the behavior of the diverse parts by obscuring activity at other levels.[23] As the organization grows and as the distance between subordinate units and those at the top likewise grows, authority leakage develops.[24] Authority leakage conveys an image of an organization that has, by reason of increased size, hierarchical authority system, and specialization, become so unwieldy that the upper levels cannot control the subunits. The organization, in short, can diversify beyond the capability of those at the top to master it.

Authority leakage allows an organizational subunit—a subsidiary, the accounting division, or the research and development branch, for example—to engage in a fraudulent transaction with another organization and ensures that no countervailing intraorganizational authority can prevent or control the unlawful behavior. Specialized knowledge further complicates this problem. In an organization with highly specialized subunits, one may lack the expertise to detect ongoing violations in another. Interestingly, subgoal pursuit and authority leakage may also lead to compliance with legal standards in the face of organization pressures to violate. Nevertheless, these characteristics also should be considered as factors that may generate opportunities for violation.

Implicit in the concept of authority leakage is that an organization should be able to control its subunits. It might be thought, therefore, that authority leakage could occur only when an organization is operating irrationally or ineffectually; that if a firm were operating in best form, information would flow smoothly (and accurately) from bottom to top and vice-versa, maximizing the possibility of control. This notion is contradicted by both research and theory.[25] In fact, the opposite has been found: information is selectively processed through the various levels of an organization as a rational strategy to protect the subunits' interests as well as to increase efficiency. The result that may in some cases be described as inefficient or irrational behavior, may thus in others be the rational institutionalization of systematic censorship procedures by those controlling the flow of information.[26]

While authority leakage is a consequence of structure that focuses attention on the inability of those at the top to control the organizational bureaucracy, systematic censorship procedures can originate at any point in the hierarchy and mask behavior throughout the organization. Units at the top may thus be encouraged to engage in unlawful conduct not only by their structural isolation, but also by systematic censorship of information that obscures misconduct from others. Furthermore, the hierarchical authority structure diffuses personal responsibility for decision making throughout the organization. Determining where within an organization a decision was made is difficult. As a result

> the delegation of responsibility and unwritten orders keep those at the top of the corporate structure remote from the consequences of their decisions and orders, much as the heads of organized crime families remain "untouchable" by law.[27]

In the Revco case, two top executives accepted responsibility for the plan to falsify prescriptions, stating no other officials were aware of the decision. Although, based on the legal concept of "the reasonable person," lack of knowledge in this case may be an explanation, no evidence was ever obtained which implicated other members of the corporate hierarchy.[28] To be sure, this may have been a case of either authority leakage or of systematic censorship to prevent critical information from reaching those with primary monitoring responsibilities, or some combination of the two.[29] Nonetheless, the example reinforces the point. The structure of complex organizations masks organizational behavior, enhancing opportunities for misconduct.

THE NATURE OF TRANSACTIONS

The nature of transactions contributes to opportunities for unlawful organizational behavior by (1) providing legitimate mechanisms that can be used to pursue scarce resources unlawfully and (2) further minimizing risk of detection and sanctioning. Transactions between complex organizations have four distinguishing characteristics:

1. formalization
2. complex processing and recording methods
3. reliance on trust
4. general, rather than specific, monitoring procedures

Though interaction between organizations may be both formal and informal, exchange has become increasingly formal, complex, and impersonal as organizations themselves have become more formal, complex, and impersonal. The massive volume and diversity of daily transactions between organizations have made rules and procedures necessary for the routinization of exchange. In the same manner that formalization develops to coordinate and control intraorganizational activities, formalization emerges as a mechanism by which organizations attempt to cope with the variety and multiplicity of interactions with other organizations in their sets. Accompanying this development has been the growth of technology necessary for recording and processing these complex transactions—accounting procedures and computer systems. Transactions are coded in special languages created for processing, storing, and retrieving masses of information. Because of specialization, both the rules and procedures governing exchange and the accounting procedures and computer systems created to keep track of transactions vary between organizations.

Although subunits within a specific organization differ in many respects, the language, transaction processing and recording strategies, and rules and procedures governing intraorganizational transactions are usually internally consistent—if not in substance, at least in form. This is not likely to be the case between organizations. Monitoring exchange under these circumstances is understandably difficult. Moreover, the ability of one organization to effectively monitor its numerous transactions with other organizations is also constrained by considerations of efficiency.

Modern society, with all its complexities, presupposes business transactions based upon a considerable amount of trust. No matter what the degree of supervisorial restriction imposed on modern employees, an element of trust must remain. If strict controls were imposed on all corporate personnel, then embezzlement, management fraud, and other illegal conduct would be greatly reduced, but very little business would be done.[30]

Because of organizational constraints to monitoring, trust thus becomes a concomitant of interorganizational exchange almost by default. Monitoring becomes a matter of observation based on sampling, tapping selected indicators, and spot checks, rather than intensive transaction-by-transaction analysis.

Considered separately, these four characteristics commonly associated with transactions may each present opportunities for illegal behavior. It is reasonable to assume, however, that the potential for violations increases when the factors combine. For example, complex methods for recording and processing transactions present opportunities for violation. Sorenson and his colleagues note how highly diversified companies with numerous businesses have complex accounting procedures which allow "creative accounting," and thus fraud.[31] The tendency of accounting procedures to facilitate unlawful behavior has been exacerbated by the advent of computer and other electronic equipment, which have come to dominate the daily operation of nearly all large organizations. While these new technologies complete and record transactions with increased speed and efficiency, they simultaneously offer faster and more efficient ways to gain resources unlawfully.

Computers are a direct link to organizational resources. Theft can be accomplished without breaking and entering. Records, secret information, funds, and programs can be stolen. Assets can be shifted from one location to another. Large amounts can be taken in minutes, or resources can be slowly drained away over long periods. The presence of the offender is not required at the scene of the offense: electronic action can happen in the future, separated by time as well as space from the action of the individual. The necessary technology, however, is not enough. Trust and general monitoring procedures will increase the probability that these mechanisms will be used unlawfully, because potential offenders weigh the risks of detection when considering use of computers or complex accounting procedures to secure desired resources unlawfully.

The factors that characterize transactions between organizations may combine in many forms to provide opportunities for unlawful behavior. When the four factors in combination repeatedly generate violations, however, then the transaction system of an organization may be said to be at fault. A transaction system may encourage unlawful behavior between organizations in two ways. First, it may directly encourage misconduct by providing convenient access to resources with little risk of detection by the other party to the exchange. Spence's notion of market signaling illustrates this possibility.[32] Second, a transaction system may indirectly encourage the choice of unlawful behavior to attain resources because the system itself blocks completion of the exchange, thus creating an impetus to search for alternative, and perhaps, unlawful methods. The Revco case illustrates this system interface problem.

Market Signaling

Spence notes that the nature of transactions inhibits an organization's ability to discriminate in decision making.[33] Organizations make decisions in a world of incomplete information gathering. Because of the number and complexity of transactions in which they engage, and the amount of information necessary to complete each one, organizations are unable to thoroughly know each individual case. As a result, signals and indexes are used as criteria to make decisions when the organization considers a transaction about which product uncertainty exists.

Spence uses transactions in the job market as an example. An employer, confronted with a pool of potential employees, is unable to gather complete information on each one in order to assess the competence of the applicant. Though the information is obtainable, in most cases the employer is unwilling to conduct a thorough search because of cost. Instead the organization relies on readily observable characteristics to make the decision. Of those characteristics that are observable to the employer, some are subject to manipulation by the individual applicant and some are not. *Signals* are observable, alterable characteristics, such as years of education, or performance, as measured by grades. In sociological terms, signals are achieved characteristics, and therefore capable of manipulation.[34] *Indexes,* on the other hand, are observable, unalterable characteristics, such as race.[35] In a competitive situation, applicants make those adjustments which will make them appear more favorable to an employer. This is called "signaling."[36] Herein lies the opportunity for fraud: some signals can be falsified, and incomplete information gathering and broad monitoring procedures may permit false signals to pass unnoticed.

Although Spence's examples are limited to individual signaling, the model is appropriate for organizations. The key elements are (1) a transaction between organizations, (2) a decision maker and a pool of applicants (organizations), (3) product uncertainty, and (4) high observation costs, necessitating reliance on signals and indexes. The delivery of Medicaid benefits illustrates the model. Medicaid services are provided to recipients through contractual arrangements between federal, state, or local government agencies and third parties (providers) for specialized goods and services to be delivered from the private sector. Organizations under contract as providers to recipients include pharmacies, dental clinics, hospitals, ambulance services, and nursing homes. To become and remain eligible to participate in the program, providers submit eligibility data (signals) on their own behalf. Because of excessive red tape, burdensome paperwork, inadequate verification of data, and poor quality control, some providers manipulate the system to their advantage.[37] Lange and Bowers provide three examples of willful misrepresentation of eligibility signals by providers.

> Major fraud and abuse occurred in the Summer Food Service Program where prime sponsors claimed to establish several feeding sites within the inner-city and these sites subsequently were shown to be duplicative. Since feeding sites are created on the basis of demographic data on potential eligible children to be served, providers would create sites on paper, never serve meals at some of the sites,

and yet fraudulently collect reimbursement for each meal claimed to have been served.

Misrepresentation of service ability may occur separately or in conjunction with misrepresented eligibility data for those whom third parties intend to serve. For example, some providers serving the Rural Housing Program for the USDA have misrepresented the eligibility of recipients. Program regulations allow providers of large housing developments or tenant housing to submit the applications of potentially eligible borrowers in a single package, thereby presenting a number of applications to USDA county offices at a time. As the program is currently structured, high volume offices have come to rely on "packaged applications" to speed the benefit delivery process. The problem is that falsified and misrepresented eligibility information which is submitted without verification is frequently taken at face value by administrative personnel.

Third parties submit eligibility data for non-existent clients they claim to serve. They then collect benefits for "ghost" eligibles. Bogus eligibility data to create a "ghost" client may be drawn from identification from the living or deceased. Duplicate social security numbers, forged obituary data, abandoned residence addresses, or falsified wage reports illustrate ways of establishing "ghosts." The Unemployment Insurance, CETA, SBA 8(a) and Vocational Education programs have documented incidences of this pattern of provider offense.[38]

To enter and remain in an exchange agreement with the welfare department, providers (organizations and individuals) have falsified market signals concerning service abilities, client eligibility, and even the existence of clients. Of course, the misrepresentation of market signals by recipients in order to obtain benefits is well known.[39] We are primarily concerned with signaling by organizations, however. When legitimate avenues to resources are blocked or appear uncertain, an organization in a market signaling situation may falsify signals in order to obtain strategic resources. Hence, the opportunities for unlawful behavior by organizations in a market signaling situation may be extended to other examples: organizations competing for government defense contracts, private firms negotiating a merger or sale, or organizations seeking accreditation or approval of a product.[40]

The Medicaid examples raise another point: false signaling may regularly occur in transactions with certain organizations. The degree to which the focal organization defines it as a chronic rather than infrequent problem might be estimated by the amount of resources the organization allocates to detect false signaling. When a focal organization is repeatedly the victim of false signaling as other organizations in its set attempt to gain resources fraudulently, the factors associated with transactions may, in combination, create a *criminogenic transaction system* in which violations are regularly produced in the course of organizational exchange.

The System Interface Problem

A system interface problem occurs when the language, rules, procedures, and recording and processing systems of two organizations fail to mesh, so that a transaction is inhibited rather than facilitated. Resource exchange may stall and become difficult to complete to the satisfaction of both parties. One or both of the organizations concerned may have to adjust their system. Negotiations may often flounder in a between-system lag induced by formalized communication. The problem may be short- or long-term, depending on the two organizations, the nature of their interdependence, their frequency of mutual interaction, the task around which the specific exchange revolves, and the resources each can devote to correcting the difficulty. Should one of the organizations be unwilling or unable to devote resources to legitimate resolution, or require immediate completion of the exchange in order to gain resources, the transaction system itself may be the chosen mechanism for bypassing the system interface problem unlawfully. The nature of transactions encourages this option, due to the low probability of detection. Another factor that may accompany the decision is a redefinition of the norms defining property rights.

Dynes and Quarantelli first explored this phenomenon in their study of organizations as victims in mass civil disturbance.[41] Organizations were selectively looted by ghetto residents. Certain types of stores were attacked, while others were ignored. Widespread looting was not explainable by objective characteristics of the selected organizations, however. Other factors appeared to be more influential in the selection process than whether the objects of attack do or do not actually have certain objectionable features. More important is how organizations, especially classes of them, come to be perceived. In essence, what appears to be involved is best described as a collective definitional process.[42]

Certain stores came to symbolize economic exploitation to the looters. This collective definition was followed by a redefinition of property rights related to these organizations. Perceived exploitation resulted in a reversal of traditional definitions of property and the emergence of a normative definition of the right to use organizational resources. Though Dynes and Quarantelli offer the explanation within a particular historical-geographic context, they suggest that the process of collective definitions and redefinitions is not restricted in time or space. Certain types of organizations come to symbolize economic exploitation, whether they actually exhibit it or not.[43] As a consequence, organizational resources are usurped. The notion is that organizations are exploitative and therefore can be exploited.

The interplay between collective definitional processes, perceived exploitation, and redefinition of property rights offers some insight into the use of unlawful behavior to resolve a system interface problem. The Revco case provides an example. Revco was engaged in exchange on a contractual basis with the welfare department, as a provider of pharmacy goods and services to Medicaid recipients. Prescriptions were given to recipients by Revco pharmacists, then submitted to the welfare department for reimbursement. That a system interface problem existed is indicated by the history of high rejection rates for Revco claims submitted to the welfare department for reimbursement. Revco was not reimbursed for filling the prescriptions which had been dispensed to recipients in the belief that the reimbursement would be forthcoming.

Recall that, according to Revco officials, the decision to falsify prescription claims was influenced by four factors. (1) They had faced this situation before. Revco had a history of stalled negotiations with the welfare department which impeded reimbursement for provider services. Revco executives believed that the corporation had repeatedly been victimized in this manner by the welfare department. (2) The two executives believed that the rejected claims represented resources legitimately owed to Revco. (3) They calculated that the cost of legitimate correction and resubmission would be more than the average amount of the claims. (4) They believed that the funds could be retrieved without being detected by the department's screening system. This belief was based on the skills possessed by the two executives. One was a licensed pharmacist and the other a computer specialist who knew the welfare department's computer system well. They thoroughly understood the intermesh between the two organizations' transaction systems. To take back resources they believed belonged to the corporation, the executives falsified prescriptions equal in number to those rejected, and submitted them through the transaction system.

The Revco case suggests that when a system interface problem ties up resources or inhibits resource delivery, unlawful attainment of resources may be a function of (1) demand for the resources, (2) legitimate access blocked by cost and delay, (3) structured opportunity to secure the resources through the transaction system, (4) low probability of detection and sanctioning, and (5) redefinition of property rights concerning possession of organizational resources. Because the Revco incident is a case study, no conclusions can be drawn about the extensiveness of the system interface problem. In exchange between Medicaid providers and the welfare department in Ohio, all providers routinely had claims rejected. This fact might indicate that in this particular welfare department, the system interface problem runs rampant. However, the department monitors the rate of provider rejection for two reasons: to work out system interface problems, and to detect fraud. If a provider's rejection rate is higher than the average for all providers, or from its own rejection history, either system interface difficulties or intentional fraud could be the explanation. The Revco case is an example of a system interface problem which led to fraud. System interface difficulties can exist without fraud, or as in the market signaling example, fraud may be the principal purpose of a transaction rather than the resolution of a bureaucratic snag.

System interface problems occasionally occur for nearly all organizations, demanding varying amounts of resources to complete transactions that stall. With transactions encumbered by formalization, complex processing methods and mechanisms, and general, rather than specific monitoring practices, some organizations may resolve their difficulties unlawfully. For some organizations, system interface problems may be the rule, rather than the exception, increasing the likelihood of fraudulent resolution. When this is the case, the transaction system itself may be labeled criminogenic.

To summarize briefly: as organizations become complex, opportunities to attain goals unlawfully multiply. Increased size, geographic dispersion, specialization, hierarchical authority systems, socialization, and internal normative environment are organizational attributes that create many locations for offenses, provide normative support for illegal behavior, and also minimize risk of detection. The transaction system provides a mechanism through which misconduct can be carried out. Offenses often are concealed by their embeddedness in the transaction system. Rules and procedures, complex methods for processing and recording transactions, reliance on trust, and general, rather than specific, monitoring procedures further encourage the unlawful attainment of strategic resources. A reasonable hypothesis would be that, as with the relationship between organizational structure, processes, and illegality, opportunities for violations will multiply as transaction system complexity increases. Thus some organizations may be more likely to engage in violations than others, depending on the complexity of their transaction system and the complexity of the transaction systems of the various organizations in their set.

This variability across organizations is important to bear in mind, for the Medicaid examples used in this chapter occur within a highly complex transaction system. Indeed, the welfare department provides a singularly extreme example: a criminogenic transaction system plagued by violations as a result of the four factors functioning individually to generate illegal behavior, as well as acting in combination to present opportunities for violations through the creation of both market signaling situations and system interface problems.

DISCUSSION

Organizations provide opportunities which promote unlawful resolutions when access to desired resources is blocked. These opportunities exist in all complex organizations operating in the legitimate economic order because of the nature of organizational processes, structure, and transactions. Created for the purpose of conducting legitimate business activity, these same factors also may promote unlawful behavior by (1) providing normative support for illegality, (2) providing mechanisms for carrying out illegal acts, and (3) minimizing risk of detection. This concealment is important, for it increases the probability that the firm's rewards for gaining resources will outweigh the perceived cost of pursuing them unlawfully. As a consequence, organizations may respond to blocked access to desired resources by turning to the opportunities immediately at hand to attain them unlawfully.

Though not all organizations experiencing these tensions will respond with unlawful conduct, these ideas suggest directions for future inquiry. This approach illuminates the importance of studying the relationship between position and unlawful conduct. Position is a key variable for understanding the response of members to the tensions organizations experience when competing for scarce resources. The skills used to commit a violation are those associated with a particular position in the organization. They are not learned from experienced criminals. They are the result of training from educators in technical schools, colleges, or professional schools. Perhaps the skills are so specific to the needs of the organization that they were learned in the organization. The point is that they are legitimate, conventional skills, not criminal skills. The technical skill for carrying out a violation is simply the technical skill required for holding the position in the first place.[44] Recall, for example, that in the Revco case one of the two executives who acknowledged responsibility for the fraud was a licensed pharmacist and the other was the former chief of Revco's computer system. Because of task segregation in organizations, however, not all members have access to the same opportunities. Not all members have equal opportunity to fix prices, to falsify sales records, to distort research outcomes, to alter plant safety standards, to package and ship faulty equipment. Because members are differentially located in the organization by position, the motivation to engage in unlawful conduct will vary, the mechanisms used in unlawful conduct will vary, and consequently the form of the violation will vary.

The social class of the individual offender carrying out the act will also vary. Business organizations are, in a sense, twice stratified. They exist in a hierarchy of organizations, and develop an internal hierarchy of their own. Thus, all social classes are likely to be represented among organization personnel. Given a situation of structural strain, organizations present opportunities for unlawful behavior that are linked to position. Consequently, organizational misconduct may reflect diversity of social class among agents acting on the organization's behalf. While social class is a powerful explanatory variable, position in an organization needs further consideration and inquiry. Both Merton's and Cloward and Ohlin's ideas emphasize the importance of social class in explaining deviant and unlawful behavior.[45] Viewing organizations in the legitimate economic order as presenting opportunities for unlawful behavior, however, leads me to suggest possible direction for refinement and extension of the work of each, based on position.

Cloward and Ohlin stress the importance of position in an illegitimate opportunity structure to illustrate the differential availability of opportunities to violate the law. However, the principle of differential availability of opportunities to attain goals illegally cannot be restricted to lower-class delinquent males—the population to which they applied their explanation. According to their definition, opportunity structures, legitimate and illegitimate, are forms of social organization.[46] In either opportunity structure, position identifies the access point to opportunities and explains the variation in mechanisms, variation in types of violation, and variation in social class of the offender.

While access to and position in an illegitimate opportunity structure may more consistently reflect membership in the lower class,[47] access to and position in a business firm creates the possibility of offenders of all social classes. While some members of the lower class may have access to illegitimate opportunities and commit illegal acts as a consequence, other lower-class individuals, because of employment in a business firm, have access to opportunities within the firm and, if subject to structural strain, may engage in unlawful behavior on behalf of the organization—thus creating the possibility that "blue-collar" as well as "white-collar" employees may engage in "white-collar crime." Position, therefore, may have greater explanatory power than social class in some instances. Research might be able to target points of vulnerability for unlawful behavior in an organization by retrospectively examining the form of violation, the mechanisms used to carry out the act, and the position of the organization member responsible. In this manner, subunits most likely to experience tensions to violate under particular circumstances can be identified and the connection between organizational strain and the internal processes generating unlawful behavior on the part of the organization can be better understood.

Merton argues that the social and cultural structure exert differential pressure on the lower class to engage in deviance.[48] A business organization is a mini-society, composed of a membership that may represent all social classes. That one strata of an organization is consistently subject to greater tensions to use innovative but socially proscribed methods of obtaining resources than others is an hypothesis that has yet to be tested. It appears to be an oversimplification, however. The idea that structurally induced motivation to engage in unlawful behavior may vary by subunit of an organization, by position in a subunit, and over time suggests greater variation than Merton originally posited. Differential pressure to engage in misconduct needs to be more fully explored in terms of position in a particular structure. Moreover, organizations themselves occupy positions in an opportunity structure. Differential pressure to attain resources and differential availability of opportunities to attain them unlawfully also need to be explored in relation to position in the larger opportunity structure of which organizations are a part. While investigating the relationship between position, opportunities, and unlawful behavior may have heuristic value for research and theory, however, opportunity is a necessary but not sufficient condition for unlawful behavior. More precise explanations will be available when the structural causes in patterns of individual choice are better understood.

6

Autonomy, Interdependence, and Social Control

Since rewards and punishments influence the choices members make on behalf of their organizations, the ability of other organizations to impose costs and, hence, restrain an organization affects the probability that available opportunities will be used to attain scarce resources unlawfully. Restraint and control, of course, occur as a condition of interaction with all organizations, regardless of role in a particular set.[1] The ability of government agencies to control illegal business conduct is of critical importance, however.

This ability is affected by the paradoxical fact that agencies and business firms are simultaneously autonomous and interdependent. While their autonomy and interdependence surely affect the full range of agency activities—monitoring, discovery, investigation, prosecution, and sanctioning—they each appear to affect particular control activities differentially. On the one hand, the *autonomy* of social control agencies and business firms seems to be a critical factor during efforts to monitor, discover, and investigate organizational behavior. Because agencies and business firms exist as separate, independent organizations, these aspects of social control activity are especially difficult. On the other hand, although government agencies and business firms are autonomous in many ways, they may become linked such that outcomes for each are, in part, determined by the activities of the other. Thus, the *interdependence* of social control organizations and business firms seems to be an important influence in the prosecution and sanctioning of suspected offenders.

Autonomy and Control: Barriers to Monitoring, Discovery, and Investigation

Organizations are, to varying degrees, self-bounded communities. Structure insulates the organization from other orga-

88

nizations in the environment. Though organizations engage in exchange with other organizations, the nature of transactions further protects the organization from outsiders, by releasing only selected information in complex and difficult-to-monitor forms. Thus, business organizations retain elements of autonomy that mask organizational behavior from outsiders as well as insiders. As structure and the nature of transactions obscure the activities of an organization from suppliers, consumers, and competitors, so do they create barriers to the efforts of social control agencies to penetrate organizational boundaries, affecting the ability of agencies to carry out their tasks.

In the Revco case, for example, the discovery of the false prescriptions was accidental; they were uncovered during the investigation of a nonrelated matter. The difficulty in discovery was a function of both the structure of the organization and the transaction system in which the false prescriptions were embedded. Revco's offense was discrete neither in time nor in space; therefore, when and where the misconduct occurred was unclear. The illegal behavior in this case is more accurately described as longitudinal than cross-sectional. The transactions which had culminated in Revco making false billings to the state had been ongoing between the two organizations for six years. The fraud itself—the creation and submission of the false billings to the welfare department—occurred over a twenty-one month period. Furthermore, the location of the misconduct was dispersed, rather than spatially confined. Organizations, unlike ordinary actors, have the capacity to act in more than one place at a time. Revco, for example, was located not only at corporate headquarters in Cleveland but in 159 retail outlets around the state during the period the offense was committed. The Ohio Department of Public Welfare similarly operated from different locations around the state.

The structure of organizations and the nature of the unlawful conduct itself seriously limit the possibility of witnesses, further impeding the ability of external authority to discover violations. The notion of a witness implies that the behavior occurs in some ways that can be seen and interpreted: a blow is struck, a gun is fired. However, the interaction leading up to misconduct in the Revco case was conducted through phone calls, correspondence, interdepartmental memos, and private meetings. Rather than a single incident, there were many, in many forms. Only part of these became permanent written record. The false prescriptions were concealed in the numeric codes of computer tapes, printouts, and claims analyses. Rather than a single occurrence, there were many instances of false submissions, mingled with legitimate transactions. The illegal behavior ultimately had to be inferred from a pattern of many, many actions and transactions, for there were no ready indicators that a violation was being committed. The financial loss to the welfare department was so thoroughly buried within the two organizations' transaction systems that it escaped even the full-time "witness" set up by the welfare department to detect fraud and abuse: the sophisticated edit programs designed to monitor use of the system.

Apparently, no witness appeared from inside the corporation to report the illegal behavior. This may be a function of unwillingness to report rather than low visibility of the offense; no data were available to shed light on this. Yet, because of the peculiarities of the offense and offender, a violation between organizations often may be hidden even from the view of many members of both organizations. When insiders do witness illegal behavior, they may see only a portion of a very involved transaction, not recognizing it as illegal because they did not see the entire transaction. The complexity of corporate law and regulations, in many cases interpretable only by experts, further complicates identification, for potential witnesses may see misconduct but lack the legal knowledge to interpret it as a violation. If insiders do witness a violation, they may seldom admit knowledge or involvement out of organizational pressure to conform, economic dependence upon the corporation, fear of being implicated, threat to career advancement, or in some cases, even to career continuation. These same factors—organizational structure, the embeddedness of a violation in the transaction system, and legal complexity—may mean that organization members participating in a violation also may be innocent of its illegal character, and thus not "witness" the unlawful conduct.

Quite naturally then, structure and the nature of transactions also obscure discovery by social control agencies, further reinforcing the autonomy of the firm. Though the state auditor's office monitored all transactions between Medicaid providers and the Ohio Department of Public Welfare on a regular basis, and the pharmacy board semiannually checked records in the individual

Revco pharmacies, the false prescriptions were not discovered by either of these systematic monitoring efforts. The proactive mechanisms developed by these agencies were not sufficiently fine-tuned to detect this particular "numbers game": paid claims resubmitted with transposed prescription numbers and changed dates. Because all organizations record transactions and thus leave "paper trails," one might conjecture that discovery would not be difficult—especially in a case like this one, where the false prescriptions continued over many months—the longer the offense goes on, the greater the possibility of detection. Yet organizational structure and the nature of transactions can obscure a "paper trail." The potential for social control agencies to discover unlawful behavior is further curtailed by the cost of expending limited agency resources for the close monitoring of organizational transactions necessary for tight control, as well as by notions of privacy.

Admittedly, discovery of misconduct may occur by means other than willing insider witnesses or the organizations officially charged with monitoring responsibilities. Though harm is frequently diffused at the individual level, resulting in a lack of reporting victims, some individuals do acknowledge their victimization by taking legal action themselves or reporting the suspected violation to an organization designated to receive complaints. In this way, other organizations may become "witnesses," bringing suspected violations to the attention of social control agencies. Other organizations may also become witnesses to possible offenses through the routine accompanying their role as supplier, consumer, or competitor. A recent example of this is an announcement by the Insurance Institute for Highway Safety, which drew attention to fiery crashes involving gasoline-tank ruptures of 1966–1973 Toyota Coronas and 1970–1978 Toyota Corollas.[2] The Insurance Institute, concerned with the welfare of insurance companies, issued a call for the government to begin a formal safety defect investigation and order a recall of models involved.

Despite the alternative modes by which violations may be discovered, however, structure and the nature of transactions so reinforce an organization's autonomy that discovery by social control agencies is inhibited. Katz suggests that the capability of external authority to penetrate organizational secrets also is affected by the nature of organizational authority.[3] Because organizations need resources from outside, development of the appearance of internal control is important. While outwardly appearing to be self-regulating, organizations protect their image by shielding members from external oversight and avoiding formal internal social control activities. According to Katz, these activities gain members' support, strengthening the organization's internal authority, but at the same time have the paradoxical effect of creating a lenient atmosphere conducive to the development of illegitimate purposes.[4]

Discovery, when it does occur, is frequently after the fact. For example, Revco's false submissions, initiated in March 1975 and continuing through December 1976, were first detected in October 1976—nineteen months after submission of the false prescriptions began. This lag between the behavior and its discovery has consequences for the investigation that follows. Social control agencies may have difficulty sorting out the facts. Documents tracing the transactions between victim and offender organizations may record only selected aspects of needed information. Evidence in written form and on computer tapes can be destroyed. Organizational membership changes.

Hence, once a violation is discovered, gathering evidence is another challenge still. The complexity and specialization of organizations and their offenses require highly specialized investigative skills. In the Revco case, no single social control organization existed with sufficient expertise to pursue the case from beginning to end. Instead, it was handled by five public agencies, which by working together increased the resources available for the investigation. This social control network is noteworthy because it draws attention to the different kind of preparedness which exists to deal with organizational misconduct: separate and specialized regulatory agencies with a potential for increased capability through resource sharing.

Even with the sharing of resources, Revco's autonomy was difficult to penetrate. The network was operating in a condition of uncertainty. The fraud was so embedded in the corporate structure and the nature of Medicaid provider transactions with the welfare department that the investigators were on unknown ground. Vast amounts of learning about the corporation were necessary to determine where and how the suspected fraud was occurring within the organization. Without benefit of access to Revco, the agencies had to accumulate information from other sources to understand organizational structure, language, technology, and transactions before they could move on to puzzling out the nature of the offense. There was continual need to rely on computer experts. Significantly, the evidence was such that its possible destruction was an overriding concern. In addition, no precedent existed for a case of this scope. The characteristics of the offender and the offense made the seizing of evidence a totally innovative procedure. Every precaution was taken to avoid technical errors which would provide Revco a loophole. Decisions concerning the seizure of evidence in five separate jurisdictions simultaneously, the use of search warrants rather than subpoenas, preparation of the documents, and execution of the warrants all were made with extreme caution.

Though the tasks defined by the social control agencies were accomplished by use of innovative methods, the specialization of business organizations and the intricacies of their offenses suggest each new case might require similar innovation. Indeed, similarities may exist across organizations, such as multiple locations and computer technology, that might generate investigative strategies similar to those used in the Revco case. Yet industries, organizations, and offenses differ. Investigation of a violation committed by computer in the pharmacy industry requires knowledge specific to that industry, that organization, that offense. Consequently, many of the skills developed by social control agencies investigating a particular offense will not transfer to future cases.

INTERDEPENDENCE AND CONTROL: BARRIERS TO PROSECUTION AND SANCTIONING

Once the specialized knowledge concerning the organization and its offense has been acquired, government agencies must integrate their prospective evidence with the language of the law: how does the organization's behavior compare with existing legal categories? A gap between legal standards and the characteristics of the offense and the offender sometimes creates problems at this stage. Issues easily resolved in traditional crime investigations may need redefinition when the suspected offender is an organization. For example, Revco's violation was not adequately described by existing statutes. Therefore, the organization's conduct could not easily be fit within punishable acts, as codified in the Ohio Revised Code.

Because the law, long oriented toward the behavior of individuals, is frequently a clumsy tool for penetrating organizational boundaries,[5] the autonomy of an organization may remain protected. However, the explanation for inadequate legal standards may rest, in part, in the interdependence of social control organizations and business firms. Interdependence between two organizations means that outcomes for each are, in part, determined by the activities of the other. When organizations are interdependent, the outcomes they reach are determined by the nature and distribution of resources between the two and the way in which the resources are used. Outcome interdependence can be of two types: competitive or symbiotic.[6]

Competitive interdependence exists when two organizations compete for the same scarce resources and when one succeeds, the other, by definition, fails.[7] A successful outcome for one implies that the other will incur a loss or forego an expected gain. Competitive interdependence applies to social control agencies and business firms in a slightly different sense. Because they are adversaries, the resources of each can be used in ways that interfere with the goals of the other. In this way, success for one may mean a loss or expected gain foregone by the other. In symbiotic interdependence, the output of one functions as the input for the other. Their fortunes are, to a degree, linked; they rise and fall together.[8] Symbiotic interdependence exists when resource exchange occurs between social control agents and those they control. Interdependence between controllers and controlled may be both competitive and symbiotic.[9] These two forms of interdependence significantly affect the prosecution and sanctioning of business firms.

Competitive Interdependence

Control efforts can become subverted by interdependence emerging from the need for social control agencies and business firms to survive in the same environment. As adversaries, the survival of each is dependent, in varying degrees, upon the activities of the other. Each thus acts to reduce power differences by efforts to manipulate and control the other's use of resources so that needs and interests can be met, and met predictably. Hence, not necessarily from concerted action, but from the activities of both as separate organizations attempting to shape their interactions with others to best advantage, a regulatory environment develops in which threat of the use of resources leads to compromise, which results in (1) compliance more often than adversarial strategies, and (2) increased interdependence of social control agencies and profit-seeking organizations.

Social control organizations possess powerful resources in the form of policy-making power, investigative and sanctioning activities. While regulation may lend certainty to a competitive environment by providing the rules for the game as well as other benefits, the possible deleterious effects are also obvious. A direct intervention by government into the firm's affairs through an investigation creates a drain on resources and personnel. Should the investigation result in formal proceedings, the organization will incur the costs of the extensive discovery, document preparation, and legal services, which in complex litigation can be staggering.[10] Additional costs may arise from the disruption of business operations, the imposition of sanctions, the negative impact on the market, compensatory advertising campaigns, public service activities, or the risk of outsiders uncovering organizational secrets. In addition to these threats an investigation poses for the individual firm, Pfeffer and Salancik note that "for many industries, governmental actions so profoundly affect their economic environment that these policies may make the difference between profit or loss or between survival and disappearance."[11]

Because a business firm's ability to survive is dependent upon the form and application of agency resources, profit-seeking organizations work to mediate power differences by efforts to manipulate and control the character of both legislation and enforcement. Shover, in his study of federal surface coal mining legislation, found strong opposition by the coal industry when Congress began to move toward new regulations.[12] The industry later stepped in, however, to insure the legislation was workable, rational, and would maintain predictability for the industry. Shover concluded:

> The history of strip mining legislation indicates that businessmen do not object to the criminalization of their conduct so much as they object to the inclusion of irrational

or incalculable elements in criminalizing legislation. When regulation seems inevitable or desirable, industry's strategies shift from trying to defeat or stall bills to assuring that whatever legislation is enacted is 'realistic and workable'—in short, legislation that is predictable in its operation and that takes seriously its interpretations of problems and priorities. At the same time, industry endeavors to socialize costs while holding control over their operations, and maintaining if not increasing options and operating flexibility. Businessmen strive to eliminate sources of unpredictability in the law, or to convert them into *administrative* problems—which can be worked out later with regulators.[13]

Of course, the commitment to such activities will vary between organizations. The degree to which organizations try to influence regulatory policy making and implementation will vary directly with the extent of dependence on the government for successful business operation: that is, it will vary with the stakes involved.[14] Despite the probable importance of dependence, organizational wealth would seem to be a critical intervening variable. To allocate resources to activities directed toward improving the regulatory environment requires, first, that resources exist for this purpose. For a small firm or a firm experiencing economic strain, resources may not exist or may exist in insufficient amounts to allow involvement in political activity with any degree of effectiveness. The inability to devote resources in this direction may be reflected in the data concerning the relationship between size, economic strain and unlawful organizational behavior. Research focusing on enforcement actions indicates that smaller firms or those experiencing economic strain are more likely to commit violations.[15] It may be that these organizations do not have a greater propensity to engage in violations, but are more likely to have enforcement actions brought because they do not have the resources to devote to shaping the regulatory environment to meet their survival needs—or they may use the resources they have in ineffective ways.

For business organizations that do invest resources toward influencing the regulatory environment, what direction might these investments take? Large firms develop internal legal departments which engage in lobbying activities in order to keep informed about potential government activities and to influence regulatory and legislative decision making that may bear upon the well-being of the corporation. Lobbying may reflect either the concerns of the single organization, or of the industry, in which case several organizations may pool resources to effect particular outcomes.[16] Formulation of legal departments should be considered not only as an attempt to influence the regulatory environment, but as a reaction to it. Legal departments inform the organization concerning laws and regulations, as well as interpret these standards as they affect company activities and policy. In this way, risk of violation is decreased, protecting the organization against direct intervention. Both the active and the reactive responsibilities of legal departments create a need for links with the regulators, and generate contact and information exchange between them.

Firms also may use resources to manipulate public opinion about the formulation of laws and regulations. Stone cites, as a classic example, the auto industry's efforts to reduce public fears concerning pollution.[17] In more direct attempts, business firms have sought to influence appointments to regulatory commissions, as well to incorporate elements of the regulatory environment into the leadership or policy-determining structure of the corporation.[18] As a result, the cross movement of personnel—the hiring of former government officials by industry and the hiring of former industry officials by government—is frequent.[19] This practice generates additional bonds between controllers and those they control. Cross movement of personnel makes sense for two additional reasons. First, personnel of social control agencies and business organizations are valuable commodities to exchange because of their accumulated work experience in bureaucracy and their expertise concerning a particular industry. In short, they know the territory. Second, agencies were created to deal with specialized problems for which Congress could not establish firm guidelines. Hence, agency proceedings contain built-in generality and vagueness. As Stone notes, "With the agencies' basic ground rules cast in terms as open-ended as 'the public interest', it is almost inevitable that the regulatees will have a disproportionately strong hand in filling in content. 'The public', whatever it is, is distant and disorganized, its interest unclear, while the regulatees are present, organized and vigilant—and they know what they want."[20]

The efforts of business firms to mediate the power of regulatory agencies, however, presents only half the explanation of competitive interdependence and its effects. Business firms also possess powerful resources which can interfere with the successful enactment of the control responsibilities so necessary to agency survival. Dependent upon federal, state, or local government budget allocations for support, government agencies strive to substantiate their existence (and their budget allotment) by conducting these activities in ways which enhance their image as effectively functioning units of government. Consequently, agencies try to minimize business organizations' use of resources that might interfere with their control activities. The business firm resources with perhaps the greatest potential to do so are information and organizational wealth.[21]

Information concerning organizational behavior is difficult to obtain, putting social control agencies at a disadvantage. Though business firms are concerned with the use of agency resources, in most cases, agencies are handicapped in carrying out control activities.[22] Oversight responsibilities are vast. Agencies, confronted with inadequate staff for inspection and enforcement, frequently must rely upon those they regulate to furnish information on which enforcement decisions will be based. Because the cost of thorough information gathering is beyond most agencies, monitoring corporate behavior becomes a matter of examining reports containing data accumulated and filed periodically by the organizations being regulated.[23] In addition, agencies have difficulty acquiring knowledge concerning recent technological developments within industries, and consequently develop a reliance on those they regulate for information on advances that might call for regulation.[24]

The need to rely on firms for information does not stop with agency monitoring responsibilities. Information gathering necessary for prosecution and sanctioning is similarly obstructed. In the face of a suspected violation, and in the absence of informants or alternative sources of information, agencies must rely on the suspected violator. Reliance on a suspected offender for information may work to the disadvantage of the prosecution.[25] In the effort to establish whether or not a violation did in fact occur, the prosecution may approach an organization early in an investigation, out of need for access to information held within the corporation. By so doing, the prosecution tips off the corporation to the possibility of impending charges, allowing the organization to monitor the investigation as it proceeds and to mobilize a defense.

At the same time an opportunity is created for destruction of evidence and cover-up. Hagan, Nagel, and Albonetti attribute the infrequency of prosecution for suspected violations by organizations to the fact that in most cases only the suspected violator has the evidence.[26] Hence prosecutorial negotiation becomes the key, and controller and controlled mediate power differences, exchanging sanction reduction for information, as a plea bargain is struck.

In addition to information, the wealth of business firms is another potential impediment to agency control activities. Organizational wealth, for purposes of this discussion, should be thought of in comparative terms. Both agencies and those they attempt to control vary in total resources, as well as in resources that can be devoted to a particular investigation. In some cases, an agency may be better able to afford the costs of investigation and prosecution than the organization suspected of violation. Should the suspected offender be a large and wealthy corporation, however, with resources over and above those of government controllers, agencies are clearly disadvantaged should the case proceed to the trial stage. Courtroom confrontations sometimes extend for years. Complex evidence, expert testimony, and multiple exhibits are costly to acquire and to present, for both sides. During the first three-and-a-half years of trial in the monopoly case brought by the government against IBM,

> the government presented fifty-one witnesses (one appearing over a month), and trial transcript totaled 84 thousand papers, and 211,000 pages of documents were received as evidence. Equally prodigious work occurred before the trial even began. The parties took over 1300 depositions. IBM is said to have produced over 65 million pages of documents for review by the government and several private plaintiffs suing IBM, and the government produced approximately 26 million pages of documents for IBM's review, almost a million of which were copied by IBM.[27]

Of course, the IBM case is an extreme example. Many agencies and many business firms could not begin to settle disputes through a legal action of this scope. However, cost is relevant with respect to possible benefits. In the Revco case, for example, cost was a factor for both parties. For the social control agencies, effort, time, and cost of a trial would add to an already long and expensive investigation. Because the case would be difficult to prove to a jury, the risk of losing was an additional cost to be avoided. For Revco, a trial was financially feasible, but would divert resources that could be employed more productively in other pursuits. In addition, the corporation wished to avoid further negative impact on the market, a possible added cost of trial.

Because social control agencies and those they control are competitively interdependent, both have a vested interest in shaping a regulatory environment which enhances their own survival. Hence, they act in ways which maximize use of their own resources to meet survival goals and minimize the other's ability to interfere. Since the information and wealth possessed by organizations can create obstacles to enforcement activities, agencies frequently fulfill their responsibilities through negotiation, internal processing, informal hearings, and mutually agreeable solutions. Business firms, similarly concerned with successful operation, soften the power of agencies by efforts to influence law making and as a consequence, the nature of enforcement, and find equivalent gains to be had from negotiating with social control agencies. Compliance emerges as a product of the power-mediating efforts of both parties, as compliance demands fewer resources from both agencies and business firms than do adversarial activities to impose and thwart punitive sanctions.

Pfeffer and Salancik note: "Organizations, to solve their problems of uncertainty regarding *outcomes* are likely to increase their interdependence with respect to *behavior,* that is, to interstructure their behaviors in ways predictable for each" (emphasis added).[28] As social control agencies and business firms work to mediate the other's power to control outcomes, interdependence increases through shared interests, attempts to negotiate, cross movement of personnel, and information exchange. In the process, the adversarial relationship frequently is compromised, and a regulatory environment develops which is as often characterized by cooperation as by conflict.

This is not to deny that in any given case a firm or agency may funnel all available resources into a full-fledged adversarial proceeding. When this does occur, however, the event will take place in a regulatory environment that has developed as a result of the competitive interdependence of controllers and controlled. The institutionalized guidelines—laws, regulations, sanctions, proceedings—have been shaped by the survival interests of both. And in many cases, these guidelines will inhibit the efforts of agencies to restrain unlawful organizational behavior in spite of skills, resources, and commitment to an adversarial stance. This is not to deny the influence of other industries, organizations, citizen groups, or the moral sentiments of the general population on the created regulatory environment. These external contingencies have been excluded from the discussion because the chosen focus here is the interaction between social control agencies and business firms, and because this relationship is known to bear so importantly on the process of social control. Outside influences have made notable contributions to the regulatory environment.[29] However, despite the creation of new agencies, changed standards, or increased severity of sanctions, the competitive interdependence of agencies and business firms will always be fundamental to their interaction. Thus, assuming scarce resources, one might speculate that the power-mediating activities of each would come into play, inhibiting restraint despite the increased potential effectiveness of changes.

Symbiotic Interdependence

Symbiotic interdependence exists when resource exchange occurs between social control organizations and those they control.[30] The output of one functions as the input of the other; the fortunes of one affect the well-being of the other. Recall that an organizational set is a number of organizations acting as consumers, suppliers, competitors, or controllers in interaction with a focal organization.[31] Each organization in the set, however, is not necessarily restricted to one role. In fact, a single organization may assume various roles in transactions with a focal organization or organizations. Or, the many subunits of a single organization may assume differing roles in transactions with an outside organization or organizations. The government, for example, while creating special units to carry out regulatory activity, also engages in transactions with business firms as both supplier and consumer. The reverse is obvious. Organizations subject to government regulation also deal with the government as suppliers and consumers. As a consequence of the exchange, symbiotic interdependence develops between social control organizations and business firms that may influence the effectiveness of restraint.

Government, as a *consumer,* engages in exchange with other organizations which supply goods and services for the operation of the government and the benefit of the public: for example, military equipment, education, highway construction equipment, research, transportation, health care, housing, office equipment. Government, as a *supplier,* provides other organizations with such resources as direct cash subsidies, legitimacy through licensing or accreditation, income in exchange for goods and services, profit protection by restricting market entry by rivals, or actions that affect substitutes and compliments for existing services.[32] According to the resource dependence model, an important restraint on organizational behavior is the dependence of one organization upon another for some resource.[33] In the absence of available alternatives for securing the required resources, the consumer organization is forced to comply with the demands of the supplier in order to negotiate the exchange.

The application of the resource dependence model to the interaction between social control organizations and business firms illuminates how exchange of resources may have important consequences for illegal behavior. Threat of withdrawal of a necessary resource is an additional sanction. When the government is supplying a critical resource to a firm, the probability of compliance with laws and regulations will be increased. And, when a business firm is supplying important goods or services to the government, agencies may be less likely to vigorously pursue compliance.

Salancik tested the relationship between interdependence and compliance by studying the response of defense contractors to the government's requirements for affirmative action regarding employment of women.[34] Interdependence was measured by the percent of a firm's sales that were made to the government (a measure of its dependence on the government) and the percent of the government's defense expenditures that went to the firm (a measure of the government's dependence on the firm). Pressure to comply with government demands was measured indirectly, based upon assumptions concerning the visibility of a firm and compliance. The more visible a firm, "the more vulnerable to informal market sanctions, thus the less likely to assume the risks of non-compliance."[35] The potential visibility of a firm to the public was measured by the dollar amount of nongovernment sales. Using these measures, Salancik found concern for affirmative action was strongly related to measures of interdependence and visibility. Large, visible firms, dependent upon government contracts, were highly compliant with affirmative action demands. Small, less visible firms upon which the government depended were less likely to comply.

The relationship between dependence of an organization on government and the probability of compliance with governmental demands receives additional support from Wiley and Zald's study of educational accrediting agencies and college compliance with agency standards.[36] The relationship between the dependence of the government on an organization and the vigorousness of government control activities gains support from the Revco case. The welfare department had the power to terminate Revco's contract as a Medicaid provider, in which event Revco would have lost annual Medicaid prescription sales in Ohio of approximately $2,000,000. Though this was considered, termination was not invoked because the welfare department was dependent upon Revco to provide services to a large number of recipients, some in areas in which other pharmacies were not available. Thus, the dependence of the welfare department upon Revco to provide services to recipients curtailed the imposition of sanctions.

To briefly summarize: the relationship between social control organizations and business firms may take two forms, which though opposite in nature, have identical implications for social control activities. Both the autonomy and interdependence of agencies and the firms they regulate will predictably mitigate social control efforts by increasing the probability that the firm's rewards for gaining resources will outweigh the perceived cost of pursuing them unlawfully, thus contributing to misconduct. Because agencies and business firms are separate, autonomous collectivities, structure and the nature of transactions mask organizational behavior—both legitimate and illegitimate. Monitoring, discovering, and investigating possible illegal behavior becomes a matter of penetrating organizational boundaries and acquiring sufficient resources to do so. Interdependence between social control agencies and business firms has its major impact on prosecution and sanctioning. Competitive interdependence refers to the potential each has, because of their adversarial relationship, to interfere with the activities of the other. To reduce this possibility, each acts to mediate power differences by efforts to manipulate and control the other's use of resources so that needs and interests can predictably be met. As a result, a regulatory environment develops in which compromise frequently leads to compliance rather than punitive sanctioning, and the interdependence of social control organizations and business firms is increased.

Competitive interdependence may become confounded by resource exchange between social control organizations and those they control. In this situation, symbiotic interdependence also exists. To the extent that a consumer is dependent upon a supplier for strategic resources, control activities may be affected. The symbiotic interdependence of the two may either increase or decrease the effectiveness of restraint. The ability to control unlawful organizational behavior may be enhanced under two circumstances: dependence of an organization on the government for resources may increase compliant behavior, and availability of alternative sources for goods and services may increase the willingness of social control agencies to act vigorously in a suspected case of organizational misconduct. Symbiotic interdependence, however, has equal potential to reduce the effectiveness of restraint. The government's dependence on an organization to provide strategic goods and services may curtail control activities, and the organization with alternatives to the government as a resource supplier may be more likely to engage in violations.

7

Epilogue:
Controlling Unlawful
Organizational
Behavior

This examination of the Revco investigation and of the broader social structure in which the event took place raises an important issue: the adequacy of resources for controlling unlawful organizational behavior. In the Revco case, an investigative effort developed in which a number of state and local agencies participated, pooling resources in order to pursue the most difficult case ever to fall within their jurisdiction. Each agency responded to its own resource deficiencies by incorporating another organization into the investigation. As a result, the sanction and surveillance technologies available for use in the investigation were expanded. Resource deficiencies still existed, however, limiting the potential effectiveness of the network. The network, moreover, was a highly specialized response that emerged because of a particular event. For another type of violation, the network's developed skills and even some of the organizations themselves would have been inappropriate.

Unlawful organizational behavior requires a specialized response. No single organization has developed to pursue all forms of organizational misconduct, as the police respond to the many types of street crime. As a result, regulatory agencies have proliferated, each with expertise in a specific area. That in the Revco case several specialized public agencies joined in a common venture to investigate and sanction a large corporation supports the frequently raised argument that despite specialization, regulatory agencies have inadequate resources to carry out their responsibilities.[1]

Part of this chapter is reprinted with permission from Diane Vaughan, "Toward Understanding Unlawful Organizational Behavior," *Michigan Law Review,* June 1982.

Many scholars and activists suggest increasing agency resources to better control unlawful organizational behavior. This
suggestion is directed toward strengthening not only sanctions
and surveillance, but the laws and regulations that undergird the
use of these technologies. Some suggest, for example, that unlawful organizational behavior be met with sanctions more appropriate to corporate actors: statutes that impose both
organizational criminal liability and personal liability for organizational conduct; statutes that more accurately describe organizational violations; greater penalties; prison sentences for
corporate executives; federal chartering of organizations; variable
fines based on gross sales rather than fixed amounts; licensing of
businessmen so that those licenses can be revoked; elimination
of "no contest" pleas.[2] Recommendations for strengthening surveillance technologies include, for example, increasing the skills,
knowledge, and numbers of agency personnel, creating laws that
require disclosure of certain information on corporate activities,
public representation on boards of directors, and mixing agency
monitoring strategies to vary the timing of surveillance for an
organization.[3]

Expanding agency resources to increase the efficiency and effectiveness of the social control of organizations has been assessed in many different ways. The records of agency
investigations, administrative hearings, and judicial proceedings
provide data on enforcement actions, consent decrees, trials, con-
victions, penalties, and other indicators that allow empirical es-
timates to be made. A realistic assessment of increasing agency
resources, however, must go beyond public records and recognize
the structural factors which affect social control. Despite increased resources, all social control efforts encounter natural constraints because of the ways in which the social structure
continuously and systematically generates unlawful organizational behavior. While increasing resources to strengthen sanctioning and surveillance capabilities may result in greater efficiency
and effectiveness in a particular case, the social structure per-
petuates the phenomenon.

For business firms, profit-maximization is a central activity and
scarcity will always be a factor. The structure of business organizations, their internal environments, and the complexity of their
daily transactions are aspects of modern life that provide suitable

opportunities for illegality. The autonomy and interdependence of agencies and the firms they regulate, moreover, increase the probability that the firm's rewards for gaining resources will outweigh the perceived cost of pursuing them unlawfully, encouraging the use of illegal solutions to business problems. Despite increasing resources devoted to social control, therefore, organizational misconduct appears to be a natural accompaniment to the complexity of business organizations and their interactions with other organizations.

It is equally if not perhaps more important to recognize that laws and regulations, surveillance, and sanctioning—the tools of control—may themselves be related to unlawful behavior. Increasing these resources to strengthen agency capabilities may have the unintended effect of increasing real rates of unlawful business conduct, even after accounting for increases from greater enforcement activity.[4] This possibility is created in a number of ways. First, the laws and regulations that prescribe and proscribe the behavior of business organizations are a major resource of social control agencies. Certain characteristics of these rules may be related to patterns of violations. For example:

1. Number: A proliferation of guidelines related to a particular industry, task, or exchange may defy mastery, or result in some regulations being selectively ignored. Large numbers of laws and rules, moreover, create monitoring difficulties, which reduce the risk of detection and sanctioning.
2. Recency: The date of origin may affect the legitimacy of a law or regulation, knowledge of its existence, or the degree to which it has been tested or officially interpreted. These factors may influence willingness to conform or deviate.[5]
3. Relevance: The degree to which a law or regulation is relevant to a particular task or the larger purposes of the organization may influence willingness to abide by it.[6]
4. Complexity: A law or rule having many interrelated parts or elements may be difficult to interpret, generating unlawful conduct out of misunderstanding.
5. Vagueness: A law or regulation that is stated in general or indefinite terms, or that is not clearly expressed may result in misconduct.
6. Acceptability: Acceptability of a rule or a law may be influenced by substantive focus, cost of adherence in terms of time, per-

sonnel and equipment, existence and strength of sanctions invoked for violation, predictability of enforcement, or any of the five characteristics identified above.[7]

Second, the surveillance technologies of social control agencies—monitoring and investigating the behavior of business firms—may also be related to unlawful conduct. Surveillance subjects an organization to accountability. To hold an organization accountable is to set up norms or criteria by which its success in goal attainment is judged.[8] Not only may this intensify pressures to attain goals, creating tensions to attain them unlawfully, but organizations may respond to the surveillance by falsifying the performance indicators being monitored. Surveillance also imposes costs on organizations. Filing, reporting, and inspection requirements for organizations demand resources that could be directed toward profit-maximization or related goals. In the event that surveillance imposes costs on organizations that interfere with other survival strategies, it may produce tensions to attain necessary resources unlawfully.

Third, sanctions that interfere with the attainment of organizational goals may operate similarly. Many sanctions seek to punish organizational misconduct by affecting profits. A business firm that incurs handicaps to its profit-making capabilities due to sanctions imposed may continue to operate with goals altered to match the reduced performance capacity, or may try to maintain its position in the competition with reduced resources. In the latter situation, firms may experience pressures to engage in unlawful conduct to attain strategic resources.

The costs of surveillance and sanctioning will, of course, have variable impact on organizations.[9] When costs are in proportion to sales or output, the impact will be the same across organizations. When costs are fixed, however, some organizations will have greater difficulty absorbing them than others. Firms not experiencing economic strain and possessing resources to adapt to regulatory strategies may escape the additional competitive pressures that social control efforts are likely to generate. Firms operating in conditions of uncertainty are more vulnerable. While all firms at times may face uncertain conditions, large and wealthy corporations can draw on greater resources should this be the case. The costs of surveillance and sanctioning technologies are thus likely to have a greater impact on small, new, or struggling firms than on large, established firms that can afford to be regulated. The greater the cost relative to net income, the greater the probability of subsequent pressures to attain resources unlawfully. Fourth, while surveillance and sanctioning may impose costs on business firms that precipitate misconduct in exchange with other organizations acting as suppliers, competitors, and consumers, the threat of agency interference with business operations also may initiate unlawful conduct between businesses and the social control organizations. To protect organizational resources, bribery may occur to ensure licensing, inspection, or contract relations that are in the firm's best interest.[10]

In a number of ways, therefore, the threat and application of surveillance and sanctioning technologies that increase corporate expenditures relative to net costs may produce illegality. While strengthening the resources of agencies may result in greater efficiency and effectiveness in a particular case, in the aggregate, greater regulatory resources may be accompanied by a rise in the rate of misconduct, in spite of the manifest purposes for which regulatory tools are created. In his research on nuclear accidents, Perrow concluded that better regulation is hard to achieve without increasing costs and risking further accidents because of imposed complexity.[11] This statement also may hold for organizational illegality. Because misconduct appears to be a function of the complexity of organizations, their interactions, and the structure in which they operate, a logical extension is that strengthening the resources of social control agencies will increase the complexity of the regulatory apparatus and thereby increase the possibility of structurally produced tensions and opportunities for misconduct. This possibility underscores the importance of distinguishing between tactics that increase the level of surveillance and the likelihood of apprehending and sanctioning and tactics that will change the corporate environment in ways that will reduce the incidence of unlawful behavior.

If the social structure produces the motivation for organizations to engage in misconduct, if opportunities to do so are ever present in organizations, if firms and agencies negotiate a regulatory environment that inhibits the imposition of costs for violative behavior, and if efforts to control violations have the unintended effect of encouraging them—what remains to be said concerning the control of unlawful organizational behavior? Does this mean that social control efforts are to no avail and should be abandoned because they only succeed in stimulating rates of corporate misconduct? While such a policy of radical nonintervention may indeed reduce the system's complexity and thus alleviate tensions to engage in unlawful conduct,[12] not to be overlooked is that agencies can regulate specific corporate behaviors. Despite the absence of long-range financial impact of the sanctions in the Revco case, for example, the system interface problem was corrected and preventive monitoring devices were installed. Any conclusions about nonintervention, therefore, are unjustifiable without an accounting of the aggregate monetary and social costs and benefits of social control and of how those costs and benefits are distributed.[13]

Some of these are difficult to assess. Recognition that unlawful business conduct is a natural accompaniment of modern life, for example, should neither obfuscate nor deny the issue of moral responsibility in the individual case. Revco had other alternatives available by which to retrieve the outstanding accounts receivable without resorting to unlawful conduct. Beyond the question of effectiveness and efficiency in the individual case, investing resources in the social control of organizations may serve an important societal function by challenging the notion of corporations as elite entities beyond the law. Another issue is deterrence. Little is known about deterrence and corporate actors. Certainly no conclusions can be drawn concerning the Revco case. Although one form of unlawful behavior was regulated for a period of one year following the conclusion of the case, the focus and time span of the research preclude any assessment of specific deterrence, and no measures of general deterrence were attempted. While it may be true that an accounting of aggregate costs and benefits of social control and their distribution is impractical or even impossible, policy should not be structured to preclude the possibility that such benefits may occur.

Rather than adopting a nonintervention stance, I offer a suggestion, based upon this analysis of the structural constraints to social control. Of the generating factors discussed in this book— the motivational impetus for unlawful behavior based on competition for scarce resources, the opportunity structure, and the autonomy and interdependence of agencies and business firms— the least addressed by scholars and activists, yet perhaps the most vulnerable to manipulation, are the transaction systems of organizations.[14] Because the complexity of interorganizational exchange has systemic consequences for illegality, reducing the complexity of transactions may also reduce rates of violations: violations emerging from transactions between business firms and between business firms and social control agencies. To realize this possibility, organizations must assume a social responsibility to recognize the relationship between transaction complexity and unlawful conduct and, hence, to monitor and adjust their own transaction systems to minimize the possibility that they are the source of violations. This self-surveillance is a dual responsibility, to be assumed by both social control agencies and business firms.

Between business firms, reducing transaction complexity may result in fewer violations by decreasing opportunities for illegality, improving the risk of detection, or by decreasing the probability of system interface problems, thus eliminating a source of motivation to pursue resources unlawfully. Because changes that decrease the possibility that an organization will commit an offense also decrease the possibility that the same organization will be victimized, resources lost to an organization in this manner can be conserved. Though one might argue that devoting resources to revamp transaction systems may create strain on other parts of the organization, in the long run savings from forestalled victimization may result that can be applied to the legitimate pursuit of organizational goals.

Reduction of transaction complexity is equally important for social control organizations. Agencies engage in exchange with business firms, as well as establish the guidelines for transactions between private enterprise organizations. In addition to their mandated surveillance activities, agencies can guard against the possibility that these regulatory efforts may generate unlawful conduct. The simplification of reporting and filing requirements for firms, for example, and attention to the characteristics of laws and regulations which may generate violations are positive directions self-surveillance might take.

For both business firms and social control agencies, monitoring the complexity of interorganizational exchange is socially responsible because it may reduce the costs of unlawful organizational behavior and its control, which ultimately fall upon the public. In addition, self-surveillance is in their own interest. Both

111

types of organizations must compete for scarce resources in order to survive. To behave in ways that create unnecessary demands on the resources available is counterproductive, because it interferes with the attainment of organizational goals. To do so also may generate tensions to attain them unlawfully.

Appendix
Organizations as Research Settings

THE DEVELOPMENT OF THE RESEARCH

Although the Revco case had made local headlines during the spring and summer of 1977, I was immersed in other work and scarcely noticed. In November of that year, four months after the case officially was closed, I had an appointment with the head of the Economic Crime Unit of the Franklin County prosecutor's office. I was looking for a dissertation topic related to unlawful organizational behavior and knew that the unit not only had data, but also had a reputation for cooperating with researchers. The head of the unit mentioned several recent cases, Revco among them. The details were intriguing. I asked if I could explore the files on the case to see if it would be a possible research topic, and she agreed.

I spent the next two months in exploratory work: talking to unit personnel involved with the case, probing files, collecting newspaper clippings, and recording leads. In many ways, it was like beginning a snowball sample: bits of information would lead to others, then to others, until the limits of the matter might be reached. In retrospect, I remember this period as one of diligent confusion. Although the files revealed the other investigating agencies involved, names of individuals connected with the case, and masses of other information, the documents and names had no logical order to me. Fearing that in my ignorance I would miss something, I took profuse notes. I organized notes, documents, and memos in files by relevant organization. I typed interviews in duplicate as soon after the actual conversation as possible, writing in personal insights and identifying issues that needed clarification.

An initial obstacle was my inability to understand the different languages confronting me. Each of the organizations involved had its own: for example, the computer language of the Division of Data Services of the welfare department (presubmission edit system, direct entry provider, error frequency analysis); the Medicaid language of the welfare department (EOMB's, claims history analysis, warrants); the financial language of Revco (8-K's, 10-K's, price/earnings ratio, operating margins). In this early phase I relied heavily upon Economic Crime Unit personnel to act as interpreters.

As I tried to order the details of the case, I felt the need for confirmation of the emerging chronology. In January 1978, I contacted the Bureau of Surveillance and Utilization Review (SUR), the investigative unit of the welfare department. The initial interview was with the person who had headed the welfare department's investigation of the Revco case. I explained that I was interested in the case as a potential research topic and described my work so far. Permission was granted to review the files and do preliminary interviewing in SUR, as well as in the welfare department's Division of Data Services.

From this interviewing and review of documents, intradepartmental memos, and computer printouts related to the case, order began to emerge. Details which first appeared ambiguous were clarified by their duplications in records of both the Economic Crime Unit and SUR. Gradually names came to be associated with particular organizations and responsibilities. The sequence of events and actors became increasingly clear as I integrated a chronological record of the case (prepared by SUR after the case was closed) with dates on memos, correspondence, official documents, and the personal calendars of those involved in the investigation. After extensive comparative documentation of the case through the cooperation of these two organizations, I concluded that there was enough information for a sociological analysis of the double-billing scheme against the welfare department.

I was excited by what I found. Although traditionally corporations have been viewed as hostile environments for research when the topic is unlawful conduct, in this case I felt that there was a chance Revco might cooperate.[1] At a subtle level, I guessed that Revco's concerns about the proposed research might be diminished somewhat by both my status as a graduate student and my sex.[2] More to the point, my preliminary investigation showed evidence that Revco did not define the act as "crime." Statements made by corporate officials suggested that the corporation saw itself as the victim, not the offender. Consequently, I felt that there might be a decreased sensitivity to the research. Moreover, the research could provide Revco with a means through which its side of the story, which had been neglected in both local and national news, could be made public.

I wanted Revco's side of the story. Inside information from a corporation charged with a crime never before had been available to sociologists. A case study seemed the natural choice to satisfy my own curiosity about the intricacies I suspected were there. The lack of monographic material on unlawful organizational behavior influenced my decision as well, for Geis's study of the 1961 electrical equipment antitrust conspiracy was the only descriptive information available at the time that had

114

been gathered and analyzed by a sociologist.[3] I was interested in the organization as the unit of analysis, and by supplementing my qualitative approach with quantitative dimensions, I hoped to develop (1) the details of the case; (2) the relations (if any) between Revco's internal structure, environment, and the evolution of the false prescriptions; and (3) the impact of the investigation, publicity, and sanctions on Revco. Revco's cooperation was essential, for I would need interviews as well as access to records concerning personnel turnover, sales, stock price, and dealings with drug distributors. However, I felt that I had two things to offer Revco that would encourage its participation: the opportunity to publicize the corporation's viewpoint in the matter, and an analysis of the financial impact of the investigation on the corporation.

Negotiating with the Corporation.

The next step was to approach Revco. In February 1978, I was granted an interview with Revco's legal counsel at corporate business headquarters in Twinsburg, Ohio, a suburb of Cleveland. At first glimpse of the building my optimism dimmed. The physical structure warned of impermeability. Amber reflecting glass covered the exterior, allowing insiders to look out, but preventing outsiders from looking in. Entry to inner corridors and offices was blocked by a reception desk, where identification badges were distributed to visitors. My arrival was communicated through the switchboard, and an escort was sent to guide me to the executive offices.

The interview was in the Board of Directors' meeting room, far from typical of the places sociologists usually convene. Although the legal counsel expressed interest, he had several reservations about the research. First, he was concerned that if I were permitted to question employees, I might include some information in my written work that Revco's competitors would find useful; for example, purchasing practices. Second, he was concerned about employee morale. The investigation, he said, had been a difficult time for the company. Uniformed highway patrol officers asking questions throughout the building had been not simply a distraction but a shock. The executives involved were longtime, respected employees. The matter had been closed, the company had returned to business-as-usual, and there was no desire to resurrect the unhappy experience. Third, he was concerned about publicity. News stories related to the case had had immediate effects on the stock price. Major stockholders, upset by the sharp decline of the stock, had personally contacted corporate executives. From Revco's point of view, nothing would be gained by generating additional publicity.

I felt his concern that I might give away company secrets to competitors was based on a misunderstanding of what sociology is and what sociologists do. I described the kind of information I wanted, how that information would appear when written, and explained that although individuals were the source of information, organizations would be the actors in the retelling. No individual names would appear. If certain information was sensitive, the research design could be tempered to meet the organization's need to preserve business secrets. His second concern, employee morale, I agreed was a delicate matter. I suggested that he act as my adviser and that together we could discuss ways to get information that would be discreet and yet still meet the needs of the research. On the issue of publicity, I told him that most dissertations are read only by the student's advisers and a loving relative or two, then spend decades gathering dust on library shelves. I did mention the practice of publishing articles from the work in professional journals, however, and admitted that this was a hope of mine. Again, I stressed the importance of the victim-offender questions raised by the case, and the sociological value of examining the relationship between these two large organizations, given Revco's victim-precipitation argument vis-à-vis charges of crime by the county. By the end of the meeting, the legal counsel had offered his personal support, suggesting that he intercede in my behalf to arrange a meeting between the corporation president, himself, and me to obtain final consent. My optimism revived.

But the promised meeting never materialized. There was never any formal statement of the company's rejection of the proposed research. Rather, long-distance phone calls to the company president were not returned, and I was informed that the matter had been turned over to the chairman of the board. I was unable to reach him by phone. I tried to contact the legal counsel with the same result. The attempt to win Revco's cooperation disintegrated into a series of phone conversations with secretaries who put me off. I could not get beyond them. This was April 1978, five months after my initial inquiry began, and a year since the newspaper headlines about the case first had attracted public attention.

At the time I explained the failure of the negotiations by my inability to convey what it was that I was about—the issue of what sociology is and what sociologists do.[4] I now question this original reasoning. It may, in fact, be true that failure to adequately describe what sociology is generates misunderstanding between researcher and subject. On the other hand, knowledge does not necessarily lessen suspicion. Sociology has a reputation for debunking, for taking sides. A promise of objectivity does not obviate this image, for objectivity might not be to the advantage of all parties concerned. Despite my expressed intent to be objective, to present both sides of the story, and to produce information useful to Revco, I believe that the corporation saw me as an adversary from the beginning.

116

In retrospect, I can see how this could be so. Although I stressed to Revco the importance of objectivity in my work, my organizational ties surely smacked of bias. I had worked closely with the Economic Crime Unit and the welfare department for three months before approaching Revco. Hoping to trade honesty for trust, I was open about this. Indeed, it was only through the exploratory work in these two agencies that I uncovered the information that led me to believe Revco might be cooperative. Nevertheless, the corporation may have viewed these previous links as suspect. In addition, I identified myself to Revco officials as a sociologist whose primary research interest was unlawful organizational behavior—a topic about which they were naturally defensive. Not only did I use this term in conversation, but the brief typed statement of research purpose I gave the legal counsel was accompanied by my vita, which mentioned previous work on "white-collar crime." Despite my honest expression of keen interest in the corporate tale of a bureaucratic financial snag that law enforcement treated as crime, corporate officials could not have been reassured by the presentation of self revealed in my language and credentials.

Moreover, I wanted to probe a recently closed but not yet healed wound, never a pleasant experience for the patient. Although I promised to conduct the research within the bounds of corporate notions of privacy and in a way that would minimally disrupt operations, I required access to records and personnel. My request and Revco's response must be viewed within the context of a pharmaceutical industry so highly competitive that entry to corporate headquarters is only through stringent screening procedures. I would argue that this predisposition to distrust goes beyond merely competitors and that Revco, in common with all profit-seeking organizations, has a particular organizational stance toward strangers—to be suspicious, to guard company secrets. The role of corporate legal counsel as gatekeeper, acting as a buffer between the organization and outsiders, reinforces this notion. Although I saw presenting "their side of the story" as an opportunity for Revco to publicly redeem itself, the corporation may have felt this to be a questionable benefit when weighed against the risk (and cost in terms of personnel time) of a sociologist loosed in the midst of the organization. Looking back, I wonder at my own naivete.

A Shift of Focus

There were five public organizations responsible for the discovery, investigation, and prosecution of Revco's false billing scheme. Two other organizations were peripherally involved, creating a massive investigative effort far beyond the official response to crime committed by an individual. This fascinated me. I decided to continue the research with a changed emphasis. Rather than focusing on the drug firm, I would center the analysis on the investigation. A study of the activities of the investigating agencies seemed particularly relevant in a society dominated more and more by corporate actors whose behavior occasionally extends beyond the reach of the law. Organizations would be the units of analyses, interorganizational relations the focus.

I would be less than honest if I portrayed this reconceptualization as influenced only by my substantive interests. I had invested five months in exploratory work, with no research funding. In addition to stifling my now full-blown curiosity about the topic, ending this study meant beginning again, delaying graduation. I was determined to complete the work. I had not given up on Revco, however. At the time, I was convinced that the corporation's unwillingness to cooperate hinged at least partially upon a lack of understanding of organizational research. I decided that when the dissertation was finished, I would send a copy to Revco. Then, for corporation officials, the sociological relevance of the case would become tangible. They would see that my intent was to be explanatory, not inflammatory. I hoped their comments and criticisms on the work would follow, and perhaps their interest in contributing the Revco side of the story would be stimulated. In either case, there was a possibility of additional information and reduction of bias.

I proceeded with the study of the social control network. My preliminary work with the welfare department and the Economic Crime Unit taught me an important lesson: as the sociologist does not understand the particular language of an organization, neither are organizations trained in the language of sociology. To avoid misunderstandings, I developed what I called the "layman's outline." This was an outline, chapter by chapter, of what I intended to write, as well as I could then foresee. It presented the research purpose in everyday language. My goal was to provide interviewees with something concrete, so that instead of raising the vague issue of what is sociology, the research purpose could be tied more narrowly to needed information and how it would be gained and used.

During the next three months, April through June, I introduced the research topic to heads of the various investigative agencies. Gaining access to these organizations was an incremental process. Since the study was to emphasize the network, if one organization refused to cooperate, the research would not be possible, or at least would proceed with difficulty. In addition, the quality and quantity of the information each divulged would affect the analysis. If cooperation were promised and restrictions were later put on information, the results could be disappointing. Thus, as I approached each organization for permission, I interviewed individuals who played critical roles in the investigation in order to tap the information available, before contacting another agency.

The Economic Crime Unit and the welfare department's SUR and data services, the sites of my preliminary work, were contacted in a more formal way than previously. I secured additional permission from decision makers with broader responsibility than those directly involved in the investigation. The early willingness to cooperate was expressed on all levels. The Ohio State Board of Pharmacy, the Ohio State Highway Patrol, and the Offices of State Auditor and Attorney General were contacted for the first time. In each agency I recounted the history of the research to date and my specific interest in the role of their organization in the case. In addition, each interviewee was given the "layman's outline" and was informed that the research would focus on the organizations involved. Therefore, no individual identities would be revealed. Several people from each organization would be interviewed to further protect the identity of those who participated in the research, as well as to increase the accuracy of the information and my understanding of the case.

The nature of the interviews themselves had changed since my early inquiries at the welfare department and Economic Crime Unit. Throughout I used an interview checklist and techniques of elite interviewing as suggested by Dexter.[5] Each interview began with the open-ended statement, "Trace the history of the Revco case and your organization's role in it." By this time, however, I was thoroughly familiar with the case, and, as the story was told, I could listen for and probe contradictions and inconsistencies. The information gathering had expanded from simple acquisition of facts to include verification by comparison; in short, analysis.

This integration of analysis with data gathering was, in part, a function of having absorbed the basics of the event, which, as in all learning, precedes sensitivity to complexity. Yet something more had occurred. In addition to the formal interviewing sessions and review of files, I had been learning in more casual ways, through opportunities created simply by my presence in the organizations: watching the routine, overhearing conversations among employees, joining them for lunch or coffee breaks. As a result I had come to know something about the stance, the motives, the world view of the investigators. This more subtly acquired knowledge increased my ability to evaluate agency interaction along with data collection—critical because data are, after all, a product of interaction.

After eight months of fieldwork, I was still unsure whether the project, as I had redefined it, could be done. Because I was interviewing in one organization at a time to test available information, gaining access proceeded in a tentative, incremental fashion. The study of the social control network was not assured until the Ohio State Highway Patrol, the last organization to be approached, granted permission and initial interviews. Ironically, the data collection was nearly completed at this point. It was July 1978.

That all these organizations agreed to participate seemed to rest on several factors. I had pointed out that their joint effort was unique and that the details of their work in this case might prove useful to other states facing similar control problems with large Medicaid providers. Agency personnel supported the need for some record of their innovative strategies as a guide for others. This reasoning was especially relevant for the highway patrol, which as a general practice avoids involvement with outside research. Furthermore, each of these organizations was extremely proud of its work on the Revco case. Contributing to the solution of the largest case of Medicaid provider fraud in the state's history had brought them all positive publicity. Contrary to Revco's fear that the research would revive a negative public image, these organizations might expect that publicity would contribute to their state and local reputations.

However, the salient factor seemed to be an extension of their participation and interest in the case itself. Even nearly a year after the case was closed, Revco was still defined as an adversary. The corporation's failure to cooperate revived feelings that Revco should not be allowed to get away with anything, including avoiding research. Those in charge of the investigation took the stance that the facts of the case should be known, and seemed to want to cooperate in compensation for Revco's unavailability. This is not to say that my access to information was unlimited. Each organization had bounds on the information that could be made public. For example, the highway patrol records are highly confidential and not open to review by outsiders. Nevertheless, each organization cooperated as fully as possible, within the limits of their own restrictions on information disclosure.

Ultimately, information came from many sources beyond these organizations associated with the investigation. I interviewed state legislators and their aides, who had reacted to the Revco case by proposing legislation requiring harsher punishment for those convicted of Medicaid provider fraud; newspaper reporters, both local and national, who had published accounts about the case; stockbrokers, lawyers, financial analysts, and accountants, who gave interpretations of the law, sanctions, and their impact.

Concluding the Fieldwork

In order to map concluding strategy, I studied all the typed interviews and marked each statement, indicating some larger category the response seemed to reflect, such as "organizational conflict." I then constructed index sheets to use for conceptualization purposes. Each index sheet served as a key to all information from typed interviews and other sources that related to a particular concept. For example, an index sheet headed "Organizational Linkages" located every statement relating to linkages that was made during interviews by interviewee, date of interview, page and line. Some remarks applied to more than one topic and were entered accordingly. Information from documents, correspondence, minutes from meetings, intra- and interorganizational memos, annual reports, appointment calendars, newspaper articles, computer printouts, and public records was integrated with interview data. This procedure allowed for the organization of masses of material and provided a mechanism for ferreting out contradictory information. Another round of interviews followed, to clarify the contradictions and fill gaps in information that became apparent through the use of the index sheets.

Though I was given permission to photocopy part of the necessary materials, most documents remained in files of the separate organizations. Therefore, a considerable part of the data gathering and some analysis were carried out within the organizations themselves. I found this to be an advantage. Not only was expert advice close at hand to interpret the records, but I could directly observe the operations of the organizations I was studying. However, when formal data gathering was completed, the remaining data analysis and writing were done away from the subject organizations. Agency personnel answered occasional questions by phone. This nine-month period of analysis and writing, which usually concludes such methodological accounts, was followed by two further field encounters: one with the network organizations and one with Revco.

Early in the fieldwork, representatives of the investigating agencies had requested copies of the completed work. Given the time they freely took from their official responsibilities to work with me, I felt they deserved to know the end result. When the writing was finished, I held a meeting to distribute copies and to provide an oral interpretation of the dissertation to aid them in translating the academic style in which it was written. For all, this was the first occasion since the conclusion of the case that they had come together; for the Economic Crime Unit and the pharmacy board, this was their first meeting. The exchange was rewarding for everyone: they were pleased that their work had interest and meaning not only to an outsider, but also to a broader audience; I found their reaction to the research an important confirmation of my conclusions, as well as a source of exciting new data.

The encounter with Revco was not as profitable. I mailed a copy of the dissertation to corporate headquarters, along with a letter asking for comments and criticisms. I stressed the sociological importance of their experience, mentioned my continuing interest in Revco's perspective on the matter, my plans to expand the completed dissertation into a book, and requested an interview. The legal counsel called me. He was generally noncommittal. He found the work interesting, but said that he was unable to respond in behalf of the company until other Revco officials had read the material. His personal feelings were that the corporation had nothing to gain by getting involved at this point. He suggested that I get in touch after the others had time to read the written work. Receiving no response to a follow-up letter sent to Revco headquarters two months later, I was left with a sense of déjà-vu.

METHODOLOGICAL ISSUES

In essence, this field research consisted of one sociologist examining an event in which eight different organizations participated, each with its own structure, history, language, and investment. In a case study which combines the structural complexity of several large organizations with a technique where the researcher is the main instrument for gathering data,[6] time and confusion have a potential for seemingly limitless expansion. Knowingly having chosen qualitative techniques, I was willing to exchange time and confusion—the known accompaniments of proceeding without hypotheses—for rich, descriptive material, unobtainable any other way. As one might expect, the combination of field research in a number of organizations and a fluid research style generated difficulties.

The thoughts that follow are my reflections on some problems I encountered in the Revco research. There were others which are not presented here—not because they are unimportant or uninteresting, but because they are familiar and many social scientists have addressed them. The methodological utility of this discussion does not lie in repetition of the familiar. It lies in the disclosure of the problems generated by field research conducted within the complexity of modern organizational life. The problems were linked to certain characteristics of the organizations being studied. Thus, rather than the traditional approach of presenting research problems in terms of stages in the research process or assigning them a genus, I discuss them within the context of the organizational characteristics from which they originated: the number of organizations, their structure, specialization, culture, public identity, admission of strangers as temporary members, and disclosure boundaries. In some instances the categories overlap. When this is the case, the problem is categorized by the organizational characteristic which appeared most influential, but the other characteristics which seemed relevant are also elaborated.

Multiple Organizations

The traditional problems of gaining access and organizing the data in qualitative research were exacerbated because of the number of organizations necessary to the study. From the literature and from previous research experience, I was forewarned about the ambiguity of collecting and analyzing masses of data.[7] Though five organizations participated in the social control network, the Revco research had two saving characteristics which minimized these difficulties. First, the event under study had a well-defined life span, and second, the focus of the network meant only specific units within each agency and only selected interactions were studied, which narrowed the task. Because of the chronology of the event, data gathering had an inherent order to it, and though I did not control the information, I controlled the flow of information collection. Clearly, the latter was a function of the research role I assumed, which was a mix of formal and informal contacts with organization members. I scheduled interviews and document research in the organizations so that I became familiar with one agency at a time, allowing myself days away from the setting to deal with organizing the data. The index sheets I devised for organizing the data facilitated and simplified analysis, because I used concepts to integrate information across organizations.

However, the difficulties I experienced securing consent and gaining access to these organizations I had neither been warned about in the literature nor predicted myself. Permission to do the research was required from each agency. Within each I found I had to contact and explain the research purpose to each individual whose position in the hierarchy had made them an authority over some aspect of the case. Because responsibility for the investigation had been scattered throughout each organization, no one seemed willing to take sole responsibility for endorsing the research project. Consequently, I interviewed (and was interviewed by) fourteen people in the network organizations to obtain permission to do the research.

Because my intent in this preliminary phase was not merely to gain access, but to determine the quality and extent of information available, I interviewed extensively in each agency before moving on to the next. Consequently, the feasibility period was greatly extended. Had I a research assistant, this phase of the inquiry could have been accomplished more quickly. As it was, eight months of fieldwork passed before a study of the network was a certainty. The ambiguity of investing time in a project which may not materialize is a problem well known among researchers. In this case the uncertainty was aggravated by my feelings of obligation to the experts who had already given time for interviews. Should the study not have been possible through the other organizations' unwillingness to cooperate, how could their contributions be justified?

Gaining access to and consent from a number of organizations was further complicated by the emergent nature of the research hypotheses, and hence, design. Wax makes the point that informed consent always is a process of continual negotiation between the researcher and the subjects.[8] Indeed, I found this to be the case. My original plans were altered four times during the course of the fieldwork, necessitating renegotiation of previous agreements with agency personnel. Each time I made a change in the research, that change had to be negotiated with all decision makers in the Revco investigation. Because the modifications in the research implied possible significant ramificiations for the agencies and agency members, I felt that face-to-face negotiation was better than correspondence. A letter provides a convenient opportunity to say "no" or to ignore the issue. The personal meetings allowed me to respond on the spot to questions, to take into account the particular concerns of each organization and each individual. The continual negotiation of consent had some obvious benefits and costs. The most obvious benefit was that it worked: the research continued with all network organizations participating. Obvious, too, were the costs: tentativeness and time. The research also may have been affected in some unnameable directions. I believe that the people felt more a part of the research process because of these periodic consultations. Perhaps the interviewees gave more time, changed the nature of the information, or took other stances, invisible to me, out of a developed vested interest in the work.

Organizational Structure and Specialization

While structure and specialization added to the challenge of gaining access to the network organizations, these two factors also produced contradictory data. Because of the specialized contributions of each agency to the Revco investigation, I found interviewees were better informed about the part of the case in which their agency participated than about others. In addition, knowledge varied by position within each organization, for responsibility for the case not only had been divided between agencies but within agencies as well. Therefore, while generally information was consistent, some details important to the research were not. These discrepancies were complicated further by the retrospective nature of the research: memories of events were blurred. In many cases, I found the needed explanation in written records. Yet sometimes the processes involved in clarification were almost intuitive, grounded in my gradually accumulated understanding of the culture and interaction of the network organizations. The question of which agency resolved the major mystery in the Revco investigation is illustrative (see chapter 1).

Interviews repeatedly confirmed the difficulty the network faced in determining how and where in Revco headquarters the false billings had originated. That the Economic Crime Unit was responsible for solving this puzzle was firmly established. In fact, the unit had preliminary notes and diagrams on file showing how they had traced the origin of the false billings within the corporate structure. However, the Ohio State Board of Pharmacy members stated in open-ended interviews that they had uncovered this information through an informant. The date they gave was early in the case—months before the Economic Crime Unit even was called in. I tried to resolve this factual disagreement in interviews in the other organizations, without revealing the contradiction I was trying to resolve. The others reported that the unit had been the organization to uncover the Revco subunit from which the false billings originated. My first thought was that my information from the pharmacy board was, for some reason, in error. I had seen the diagrams in the Economic Crime Unit files, heard descriptions of how the unit had pinpointed the Revco department responsible. I wondered if the discrepancy was simply a matter of forgetting over time. The pharmacy board's participation had been intense. Nonetheless, recall of who did what may have become confused. An alternative explanation was that I was being intentionally misled.

On the pretense of discussing another matter, I arranged a group interview at the pharmacy board. During this meeting, I asked for further details concerning the board's role in determining how and where in Revco the false billings originated. The board stated that since the information came from an informant, they would be cautious in the discussion in order to protect their source. However, board members referred to files in my presence (though I did not read them) and agreed upon dates and descriptions of events. I was convinced that both organizations, working alone, had figured out where in Revco the fraud had occurred. Since this knowledge was critical to the investigation, why hadn't it been forwarded to the prosecutor's office, which held the responsibility for concluding the investigation? The solution finally came when I realized that of the five organizations involved, the unit and the pharmacy board were the only ones that had not directly interacted before or during the investigation. The pharmacy board's major work was complete before the unit was called in (see table 2). It was quite possible that both had pinned down the department and the individuals within Revco responsible for the false billings, but without contact with each other, and without a linkage between the two organizations, the information was never passed on. This was an important finding concerning the operation of the social control network.

In the above illustration, the source of contradictory data lay in the structure and specialization of the network. These same factors generated discrepant information within the individual organizations. Specialization resulted in tasks and knowledge being lodged in various layers of an agency. The resources and skills of each of these subunits were highly particularistic, as were their functions in the investigation. As a result, flow of information between them was obstructed. Thus, to varying degrees organizational structure and specialization insulated the network organizations from one another, and insulated subunits within the same organization as well, producing a capacity for misunderstanding, partial truths, and hence, contradictory data. Other explanations exist for discrepant observations,[9] yet a sociologist of organizations would be remiss not to take into account the possibility of a structural one. Whatever the explanation, the researcher's ability not only to discern but to unravel contradictory data is a matter of gradually developed understanding of contextual contingencies: in this case, a mental flowchart of the units of the larger organizations, the nature of exchange between them, the allocation of responsibility among personnel, division of labor, and, perhaps more important, attunement to the world view of those who participated in the event being studied. In other words, the researcher must become sensitive to organizational culture.[10]

Organizational Culture

Each organization has its own culture, characterized by a unique language. The ability of the researcher to understand the culture and its language is critical to data gathering and analysis, for both involve discrimination and interpretation. In *Street Corner Society,* Whyte cited this classic problem.[11] He spent months in the research setting before any discernible order began to emerge, and he relied heavily on his informant to interpret the norms and language of the subculture he studied. I experienced these same difficulties, discovering that the inability to discern relevant information initially stimulated overlearning. In the Revco case, I spent hours on manuals, reports, and computer printouts that shed very little light on my specific research topic, but did give a better understanding of the world in which I had temporarily placed myself. The development of good rapport with experts in each network organization who could act as my interpreters was absolutely essential. I found it necessary to rely on experts from other organizations as well, first, because my training had not prepared me to understand and interpret certain information commonly understood by those who frequent the realm of the large organization, and second, because I wanted to weigh the information from insiders against information from outsiders.

My greatest handicap became apparent during the study of the impact of sanctions on Revco. The ability to do a market analysis was not in my repertoire. I asked a certified financial analyst to compare Revco's stock prices and price/earnings ratio with three other comparable retail drug chains over the same period.[12] Without her contribution, I could not have discussed the impact of the investigation on Revco in anything but superficial terms. But this was not the extent of the help required to evaluate the interactions of these complex organizations. I called upon others—journalists, lawyers, pharmacists, accountants, legislators. Yet a caveat is in order. Though one can rely on experts for interpretation, the researcher must still learn the culture and its language sufficiently to evaluate and put to use the information received from others.

126

Even though culture and language become sufficiently mastered, the stubborn problem does not abate. This learning is rarely transferable. Industries and organizations are unique. Hence, learning the culture and special vocabularies associated with one organization, or with one substantive research question related to organizational behavior, does not necessarily transfer to others. Moreover, the language problem must be conquered anew when communicating research results. The ultimate irony of the learning of these languages is that once mastered, the researcher, without pause, adopts them. With the strangeness of the newly learned jargon gone, the researcher (now writer) tends to write assuming a level of understanding that the audience may not possess.

The Public Identity of Organizations

Traditionally, the identity of the research subject is concealed. I began writing using a pseudonym for Revco, in keeping with the traditional approach. However, as work proceeded, I began to question my original decision. Should I also use the pseudonym in the footnotes which referred the reader to annual reports and headlines? If I used the pseudonym in the footnotes, anyone looking up the citation could learn the corporation's identity. On the other hand, using the pseudonym meant in some cases an interested reader could not confirm the data because the source could not be located without the corporation's name. Should I use the pseudonym throughout the text, while using the true name in the footnotes to properly document the facts? This made the use of a pseudonym at all seem an absurd disguise. Or should I conceal Revco's name both in text and citations, thus concealing the corporation's identity, but diminishing the scholarly quality of the work?

The question of proper identification of organizations was not restricted to Revco. There was a similar decison to be made concerning the network organizations. The analysis centered around organizations as actors, rather than individuals. Several people in each organization were interviewed to increase the accuracy of information as well as to insure that no one individual could be singled out as the source. I promised confidentiality to those who were interviewed. However, if in text or footnotes, I identified state and county (Ohio Department of Public Welfare, Franklin County Prosecutor's Office), individuals responsible for the investigation would be identifiable because of their public association with a particular agency. Moreover, because of the national publicity accompanying the case, once the state was known, Revco's identity would be known. A further clue to the identity of all the organizations was my academic affiliation, which was in the same city in which the investigation originated.

I decided that there was little chance of concealing the identity of the several organizations involved, no matter how I proceeded, because of the public nature of the organizations and the Revco investigation. I recontacted each person interviewed in the agencies to discuss my changed stance, for I felt their opinions about naming true organization names should be taken into account.[13] Though the research focused on organizations, it was still a study of human performance. Ultimately, individual identities were at risk. I warned them that though I would use only organization names, I could not guarantee individual anonymity because of the public nature of their responsibility. With their consent I decided to próperly identify all organizations in the text and properly document information through fully identified footnotes. Individual sources would be carefully guarded.

These are my reasons for this decision. First, the case was a matter of public record. Documents and information were available to anyone who inquired. Second, with the exception of Revco, the organizations involved were all government agencies. Their social control responsibilities were well known, and their role in the Revco investigation well publicized. Third, all too often, sociologists have focused on the behavior of society's outcasts. Rarely has research extended to the deviance of the privileged. The scarcity of this type of information demands the most careful, accurate documentation possible.

Researcher as Temporary Organization Member

Most organizations have mechanisms for admitting strangers into their midst on a temporary basis: prisons provide for volunteer groups, hospitals for visitors, universities for visiting fellows, corporations for consultants and IRS investigators. In exchange for a display of credentials, the organization assigns a newcomer a position which entails certain rights and obligations. Not all who are admitted temporarily, however, become temporary organization members. This form of admission implies something more than a guest lecture or a visit to a sick friend. This implies a period of continual exchange: a pattern of interaction between the newcomer and the organization. A researcher doing fieldwork in an organization interacts regularly with members, and thus becomes a temporary organization member.

Natural bonds are formed when a researcher remains in any setting for a length of time. In the Revco research, interviews and discussions in the network organizations continued over many months; I came not only to respect organizational expertise, but also to form friendships and loyalties. Yet the many advantages of my acceptance were not without complication, for this bonding generated a series of difficulties.[14] Though individually unique, these difficulties were linked because the bonding that accompanied my becoming a temporary organization member was their common source. They shared a common resolution, as well.

Sometimes, in this profession, the resolution of research problems comes by a martialing of forces and by direct attack; sometimes they are resolved by happy accident; sometimes they simply remain unresolved. In this instance, resolution falls clearly into the "happy accident" category. It is only in retrospect that I can see how this occurred, and I mention it now in the hope others may find the technique useful when organizations are the research setting. You may recall that I held a meeting to review and distribute the completed dissertation to representatives of all the network organizations. This meeting at once solved the three problems that I attribute to becoming a temporary member of these several organizations: conflicting loyalties, leaving the setting, and dissemination of information.

Conflicting loyalties. On several occasions, representatives of one organization were critical of decisions made by another organization during the investigation. The criticisms were raised because the rationale for investigative tasks handled autonomously by an organization were not routinely shared with all network organizations. In interviews, I had heard the rationale behind these decisions. I felt strong urges to correct what I saw to be misplaced blame—that is, to justify the behavior of one organization to another. The desire was greatest during an interview, when criticisms were raised. Because I wanted to minimize my impact on the situation I was studying, I did not speak up. Nonetheless, when later working in the organization which I felt to be unjustly accused, I felt uncomfortable for not having done so.

The meeting to discuss the research findings allowed these unspoken disputes to be settled directly, without betrayal of confidence on my part. Representatives of all the network organizations assembled in a university seminar room. In this setting, I was speaking solely in my professional role. I described the research results. At one point, I introduced the misunderstandings between the organizations as a problem of network communication. The response was immediate. Those who during the investigation had made decisions which seemed controversial to the others voluntarily discussed their rationale with the group. This settling of issues occurred in part, I feel, because the discussion that day focused not upon the individual organizations, but upon the network. I believe the people there, professionals who cared very much about their work and the case, took that as their charge. Furthermore, part of the explanation may lie in the creation of an arena where information could be objectively and dispassionately exchanged. Whatever the full explanation, the effect of these disclosures was to dispel hard feelings and cement relations between organizations.

Leaving the setting. There was an awkwardness about terminating the bonds formed in the research settings, for my interest in and liking for the people I met in these agencies was genuine. Yet my physical absence from their work world meant that the relationships could not be continued as easily. I did not want them to feel that my friendship had a purely pragmatic basis, for in fact it didn't. Yet, because of the need to write and other obligations, I was initiating these contacts less and less. The problem was one of redefining the relationships in a mutually satisfactory way. The same meeting also resolved this problem. Ambiguity had surrounded my friendships with organization members since I first left the setting at the beginning of the analysis and writing period. The discussion of the completed research was like a closing ceremony. The work was discussed; loose ends were gathered in. There was a moment when all of us tried to express our mutual respect, gratitude, and best wishes for the future. It was clear that we would all return to our separate worlds. Each left with a copy of the dissertation, promising to relay to me any additional comments. Initiation of the next contact clearly rested with them. My responsibility had formally ended.

Dissemination of information. When I first contacted each network organization, I presented the need for outsiders to know their investigating strategies as a reason for cooperating in the research. I pointed out the practical utility that techniques used in the Revco investigation would have for other states investigating large cases of Medicaid provider fraud. When the research was completed, I felt conveying the research findings to others was a promise I was obliged to keep. A dilemma surfaces in the necessary trade-off with professional mandates that this activity brings. As sociologists, we are not rewarded for disseminating information to those in the real world who can apply it. We are rewarded instead for publication in scholarly journals. Time spent in one direction is time taken from the other. How do we meet our obligations to disseminate our research findings to audiences beyond our discipline and at the same time satisfy our need for professional self-perpetuation?

Since this now-fateful meeting, I no longer see this as a dilemma of mutually exclusive choice; I have recast it, in fact, as a nondilemma. The pursuit of professional goals can be enhanced by time spent disseminating information to those whom it directly affects. The meeting with the network organization members, which, at the most, required two days of arrangements and preparation, directly enriched my own professional interests in several ways. The immediate feedback was invaluable. The conversation confirmed the research conclusions, as well as generated ideas for additional work.[15] In addition, I received the latest information from these experts on new legislation, political activities, and prosecution efforts that affected their work on Medicaid provider fraud. Having withdrawn from day-to-day contact with these organizations some nine months earlier, I was unaware of the consequences of these new developments for the network.

The outcome of this meeting was so overwhelmingly favorable that I followed through on my original promise with no second thoughts. After an initial inquiry on my part was followed up by HEW, I agreed to meet with officials responsible for control of Medicaid fraud and abuse in Washington. Though no money was to change hands, I knew the exchange would be professionally valuable: there would be new ideas, and perhaps a foundation laid for a broader study of networks as a device for social control. Tangible benefits to one's own research and research interests can come from sharing information with people outside the profession who find it relevant. However, there is another factor to support such activity: the more relevant our work is to the practical problems of the organizations we study, the more agreeable those organizations will be to researchers who might later want their cooperation.

Disclosure Boundaries

Every organization has established boundaries for disclosure of information. In this research, I found these boundaries varied from Revco's absolute impenetrability to an almost open-door policy in some of the other organizations. In between these two extremes were various limitations on certain types of information within particular organizations. In part these boundaries were determined by whether the organization in question belonged to the public or private sector. In part, they were determined by the roles the various organizations played in the case: the investigator or the investigated. The shaping of these boundaries simply cannot be attributed to any single factor, however. All organizations have disclosure boundaries defined by law, regulations, and norms which channel interaction between the organization, its members, its clients, and the general public. Yet the nature of the organization, its goals, and the kind of information needed to achieve them all contribute to the information limits set in a particular instance. Whether or not the researcher ultimately gains access to desired information depends upon the interweaving of these factors—an interesting and unpredictable dynamic. In studying unlawful organizational behavior, the sensitivity of the subject matter further reduces the permeability of routine disclosure boundaries. Sociologists, moreover, must contend with barriers to information imposed by the ethical requirements of their own discipline.

My response to Revco's unavailability was to turn to other sources to obtain information. Although the sources were varied, I relied primarily on interviews and documents originating with the agencies responsible for social control. I used whatever information was legitimately available to reconstruct Revco's position. Nonetheless, the result is still a one-sided story—a story developed from information obtained from the investigating agencies. These agencies all shared the same world view.

Organizations are seductive.[16] Becoming a member, however temporary, of an organization to study a particular event is akin to participating in the event itself. The possible biasing effects of this type of affiliation are difficult to sort out at the time. The research problems I noted above— conflicting loyalties, leaving the setting, and dissemination of information—all reflect attachment to network organization personnel and hence, raise questions about the reliability and validity of the data.

I began this project fully aware that my sympathies lay with my own kind: the average citizen, a good part of whose life is dominated by decisions made in some far-off executive suite and who suspects (sometimes accurately, sometimes not) that they are being taken advantage of by large organizations on a daily basis, in some unknown and uncontrollable ways. Thus the issue for me, in Becker's terms, was not whether or not I had "taken sides," but whether the taking of sides meant that some distortion was introduced into the work so great as to make it useless or invalid.[17]

I felt this knowledge of my personal bias a decisive factor in being able to limit its influence on my work. I purposefully directed the research in certain ways to compensate for it. In fact, my first attraction to the Revco case as a topic was exactly because it contradicted my bias: here was what looked to be a case of a corporation getting ripped off by the system. And, though Revco was not available, I pursued that line of inquiry. Further, the awareness of my bias influenced my continued attempts to engage Revco in the project as well as to balance my presentation of the findings to network members and HEW staff by sending a copy of the dissertation to Revco.

Despite awareness of my bias and my attempts to direct and control it through the use of systematic research practices, indications of my personal leanings appeared in the dissertation in ways I did not perceive at the time. In fact, it has only been since then, through the gradual process of rethinking and rewriting the manuscript, that I became aware of possible distortion. I first became suspicious that my social control affiliation had an unknown influence on my work as I noticed subtleties in the language I had used in the dissertation (for instance, describing Revco as "the criminal corporation" early in the chronology of the investigation, before this was proven).[18] Several revisions and re-examinations of the work leave me confident that the facts of the case and the analysis are accurate and useful and I am content to let them stand. Yet after-the-fact discoveries of bias disturb me. Not that a researcher's viewpoint should not be integrated into the work, but it should not be unknowingly integrated. In my case, only over time and with the task of revising and expanding the dissertation into a book was I able to recognize the degree to which I had been captured by my affiliation with the network organizations. Each succeeding draft could be treated as data reflecting my social and professional distancing from my research subjects, and thus my increasing objectivity.

Yet retrospective analysis and revision of an already completed work are infrequent luxuries. The researcher needs a heightened sensitivity to biasing influences while the work is going on. Because any fieldwork affiliation with an organization or several organizations with similar world views contains a potential for bias, the researcher should take precautions that these natural biasing influences do not become unwittingly incorporated into the work. Of course, reliance on the tools and techniques of the discipline to insure that the research meets the standards of good scientific work goes without saying. But in addition, the researcher can incorporate strategies into the investigation that specifically monitor developing biases by forcing the researcher into regular confrontation with other worlds than the one being studied.

Systematic generalization may help to alert the researcher to the biasing effects of an organizational setting. The primary purpose is not ultimately to generalize, but to free the researcher's mind from total occupation with the intricacies of the case at hand and the culture of the organizations temporarily joined and to force considerations of broader scope; hence, "generalization." To effectively keep the researcher in touch with bias, moreover, these procedures should be integrated into the research process at scheduled intervals; hence, "systematic." Systematic generalization consists of three procedures: *collegial exchange,* which allows the researcher to maintain perspective on self in relation to the research setting; *outsider interviews,* which allow the researcher to know the setting or event from the perspective of others in the organization's environment; and the *comparative method,* which allows the researcher to know the setting or event as it compares with similar settings or events.[19]

Collegial exchange. Leaving the setting is one solution commonly suggested as an aid to maintaining objectivity during fieldwork.[20] Leaving the setting implies that the researcher has been separated from the influences of the setting. Merely leaving, however, is insufficient, for in many senses, the researcher can take the setting along—the hypotheses, the data, the ongoing analysis. Then, although the researcher does analysis and writing in isolation, any biasing influences of the setting are likely to be perpetuated. A true separation occurs when the researcher can be reflexive about that "other self"—the field research identity. (By field research identity, I do not mean a sociologist who has assumed a covert research role. I mean any researcher, who in a research setting, adopts aspects of the world view of those being studied.) This reflexivity is facilitated by periodic relocation in another setting that confirms the

Appendix

identity of the researcher qua researcher: an academic setting or work location where the researcher is surrounded by professional colleagues. Yet this in itself is not enough.

Collegial exchange is essential. The creation of a seminar environment, in which a small group occasionally can discuss the analysis, is preferable. Formalized to this minimal degree, collegial exchange not only confirms the professional identity of the fieldworker, but it also provides an arena where the ongoing mental processes of analysis can, at regular intervals, be made public and considered by others not seduced by the particular organization or event that naturally becomes so central to the fieldworker's life.[21] The subtle acquisition of bias may be exposed. And, by enhancing professional identity, regular collegial exchange maximizes the possibility that the researcher will re-enter the field with a renewed sense of autonomy in relation to the research subjects, thus increasing the researcher's ability to know self in relation to those being studied. For the sociologist working alone in the field, the integration of collegial exchange with the ongoing research is a key mechanism for sensitizing the researcher to unknown bias acquired in the setting. This may also be an important strategy for a team of field researchers. Though regular exchange among them can provide a check on biasing influences, the group can evolve premises that reflect the effect of the organizational setting on the group as a whole. In many cases leaving the field means adjourning with others involved in the project. Thus, the seductive effects of the setting may be taken along, remaining hidden, unless regular exchange with noninvolved sociologists or interdisciplinary specialists is sought.

Outsider interviews. In order to evaluate data, the researcher must not only be informed about the context, but must know thoroughly the source of the data, must wonder why the organization or individuals agreed to cooperate, must consider how information was selected to give the researcher. Because all organizations have bounds on the information that they disclose to researchers, these questions must be systematically raised through all phases of the research process. Though the researcher's knowledge of the subject's world view may lead to formation of tentative conclusions, seeking outsiders may produce additional insights that aid in discovering biases inherent in primary data sources.

Outsiders are individuals informed about the subject matter who, because of position within the group, in another group, ideology, occupation, or even varied proximity to the event or setting, may hold different perspectives than the primary data source, the participants in the organization or the event itself. Outsider interviews allow the researcher to know the organizational setting or event from the perspective of others in the environment. When scheduled at regular intervals, these interviews cause the researcher to periodically leave the field and attend to alternative viewpoints. Files can be constructed and this information from outsiders reviewed periodically as the investigator proceeds, because data that at one point seem to be useless, at another point can appear quite relevant, and the researcher is reminded of other perspectives even when contacts with outside sources are finished. Outsiders, of course, have their own biases; thus, it is important to consult as many different informed sources as possible. In the Revco case, legislators, newspaper reporters, and members of noninvolved social control organizations served as my outsiders. Through them, I was able to verify and challenge existing data and emerging explanations. Knowing the network organizations and the event within the context of the environment aided me in identifying external contingencies that shaped organizational decision making.[22] I was able to put the case in political context, an impossible task with information only from the network organizations.

The comparative method. Glaser and Strauss have urged the utility of a comparative method for development of substantive theory from field research.[23] To test developing hypotheses and explanations, a particular case is examined against others, either studied in the field or through library documents. Their point is that contradictory instances and alternative hypotheses, as well as confirmation of patterns in the case at hand, can be found through systematic comparison with other cases. I suggest that in addition to facilitating theory development, the comparative method forces the researcher to maintain a keen sense of the idiosyncratic qualities of the organizational setting. This heightens sensitivity to the biasing influences of the setting, whether the goal is theory formation or analytic description. Comparison cases may be quickly acquired through historical documents or other written materials.[24] Their examination should be accompanied by recording of similarities and differences between the case at hand and other instances of phenomena in the same class. With careful inspection and careful record keeping, the researcher can keep in touch with the idiosyncratic characteristics of the research setting, minimizing the impact of the setting on the ongoing analysis.

Because data gathering and analysis are simultaneous and hypotheses are frequently emergent, I suggest that systematic generalization occur at established time intervals convenient to the scheduled work in progress. Of course these suggestions will need to be tempered to fit the problem being studied as well as the number of researchers participating, but the intervals should be frequent enough that bias developing in the research can be monitored. Though in the long run we can seldom give a balanced picture, taking precautionary steps such as these will increase the validity and usefulness of the finished work.

CONCLUSION

Those who conduct organizational research should be sensitive to the possible connection between organizational characteristics and the research process. Though the difficulties mentioned on these pages arose in conjunction with a specific research project on an organizational network, unlawful conduct, and social control, they may be counted on to occur whenever a complex organization is the research setting and the method is qualitative.

Moreover, some of these organizational characteristics may generate similar problems for quantitative research in organizations: structure and specialization may complicate gaining access and data analysis; culture and language may be critical to instrument preparation; the public identity and documentation issues may require resolution. To determine the extent to which these problems generalize, other research, both qualitative and quantitative, will need to be assessed in terms of these and perhaps additional organizational characteristics. But forewarned is not necessarily forearmed. In some cases the methodological difficulties associated with particular organizational characteristics may be unavoidable. Nonetheless, perhaps they can be studied as they unfold, enriching organizational theory as well as research methods.

Notes

INTRODUCTION

1. Andrea G. Lange and Robert A. Bowers, *Fraud and Abuse in Government Benefit Programs* (Washington, D.C.: Department of Justice, Law Enforcement Assistance Administration, National Institute of Law Enforcement and Criminal Justice, 1979), p. 24.

2. Ibid., pp. 13–40.

3. See, for example, "Fraud and Abuse Are Twin Plagues of Welfare," *Nation's Business* 67 (January 1979): 38; Byron G. Lee, "Fraud and Abuse in Medicare and Medicaid," *Administrative Law Review* 30 (Winter 1978): 1; "Computer Uncovers 13,584 Collecting Double Benefits," *New York Times*, 8 February 1978, p. 8.

4. James S. Coleman, *Power and the Structure of Society* (Philadelphia: University of Pennsylvania Press, 1974).

CHAPTER 1

1. Most of the data in this chapter were confirmed by documents and interviews from all five agencies participating in the investigation. When a statement was verified by multiple sources, the sources are not identified. When the information came from a single source, however, the origin is specified in a note. The highlighted dates identify events that I defined as turning points in the Revco investigation: the initiation of a new investigative phase, the inclusion of a new organization, or a significant finding. Documents or interviews in all agencies confirmed that the events occurred on these dates.

2. Ohio Department of Public Welfare, interdepartmental reference, 27 April 1977.

3. The image of the state highway patrol as an organization whose sole responsibility is policing the highways is inaccurate. In Ohio, the patrol has full police powers to investigate any criminal act on state-owned property. In addition, the patrol may pursue any criminal investigation which involves state property interests. Therefore, the organization has the authority to investigate welfare fraud cases. In fact, in

November 1976, without knowledge of the still secret Revco investigation, the Ohio governor ordered a task force of state highway patrol officers to investigate welfare fraud. A unit of five troopers was stationed in the building which housed the Ohio Department of Public Welfare, as well as other state offices, for this purpose. By April 1977, when the pharmacy board called the patrol into the investigation, it had some experience with welfare fraud, in addition to possessing the jurisdiction to pursue the case in all suspected Revco stores around the state.

4. The Economic Crime Unit was formed in 1973 as part of a federally funded National District Attorneys' Association project to improve investigation and prosecution of white-collar crime. At the time of the Revco investigation, these special prosecution units were attached to fifteen county prosecutor's offices in major cities throughout the United States.

5. Search Warrant Affidavit, 27 April 1977, p. 3.

6. Ohio Department of Public Welfare, interdepartmental reference, 27 April 1977.

7. *Columbus Dispatch,* 29 April 1977, p. 1.

8. Revco Drug Stores, Inc., interoffice communication, 18 May 1977.

9. Ibid.

10. Ohio Department of Public Welfare, intraoffice communication, July 1977.

11. Interviews, Ohio Department of Public Welfare, Division of Data Services, 18 July 1978.

12. Interview, Ohio Department of Public Welfare, 18 July 1978.

13. Interview, Revco Drug Stores, Inc., February 1978.

14. *Wall Street Journal,* 1 August 1977; Interview, Economic Crime Unit, 9 May 1978; Interview, Ohio Department of Public Welfare, Division of Data Services, 18 July 1978.

15. Press release, Franklin County Prosecutor's Office, Economic Crime Unit, 29 July 1977.

16. Ohio Department of Public Welfare, Division of Medical Assistance, Bureau of Surveillance and Utilization Review, *Preliminary Report of Examination of Provider Records: Revco Drug Stores, Inc.* 1977. The discrepancy between the number of claims and amount of the loss indicated here and the figures mentioned other places in this chapter occurs because the welfare department revised its technique for calculating these figures as the investigation progressed. See note 20.

17. Lynn A. Oberg, "The Effect on the Price Movement, Earnings, and Price/Earnings Ratio of Revco Drug Stores and Other Selected Drug Retailers of the 1977 Medicaid Fraud Investigation and Settlement," in Diane Vaughan, "Crime between Organizations: A Case Study of Med-

icaid Provider Fraud" (Ph.D. dissertation, Ohio State University, 1979), pp. 190–200.

18. Interview, Revco Drug Stores, Inc., Twinsburg, Ohio, February 1978.

19. Interview, Ohio Department of Public Welfare, Division of Data Services, June 1978.

20. The complexity of the plan is indicated by a listing of precautionary steps accompanying implementation of the system:

1. Each step required that the input be read in a different sequence.
2. As each successive stratification (type of overpayment) was extracted, it was copied to one tape file and those remaining claims copied to another file.
3. The latter was used as the input to the next step to ensure that a claim record would not be selected for more than one error group.
4. Each step, in addition to writing the two tape files, printed a report of the claims paid in error and the momentarily "valid" claim which conflicted with each, a count of the claims paid in error and the dollar amount of those claims. See *Highlights of Revco Drug Stores, Inc. Investigation,* Files, Ohio Department of Public Welfare, Bureau of Surveillance and Utilization Review, 1977.

21. The Ohio Department of Public Welfare acknowledged these difficulties in their preliminary report. In regard to their method, they stated:

> It is recognized that such a method will not recover all claims that are in error. Indeed, it is conceivable, moreover likely, that not all of the error types have been identified. Similarly, it is conceivable that, for a number of reasons, a valid claim may have been extracted as an invalid claim. It is economically infeasible, however, to eliminate the factor of human error, either clerical or interpretive, from this study. It must be noted at this point, in contrast, that the elimination of such errors is entirely possible and that the Ohio Department of Public Welfare is fully prepared to do so to the limits of legal and scientific infallibility. (*Preliminary Report of Examination of Provider Records: Revco Drug Stores, Inc.,* p. 2.)

22. Prior to the Revco case, the welfare department had established a pattern of referring Medicaid provider fraud cases needing legal action to the attorney general's office. That office would then bring a civil suit against providers under the federal False Claims Act of 1863. Unless a case was referred by the welfare department, the attorney general's office had no jurisdiction. In the present investigation, the highway patrol referred the case to the Economic Crime Unit of the county prosecutor's office because it had the authority to prosecute criminal cases, rather

than referring the case to the attorney general's office, which was without criminal prosecution powers. (See 31 USCA 232.)

23. *Wall Street Journal,* 8 July 1977.

24. Theft by Deception, Ohio Revised Code 2913.02(A) (3): "(A) No person, with purpose to deprive the owner of property or services, shall knowingly obtain or exert control over either. . . . (3) by deception." Falsification, Ohio Revised Code 2921.13(A) (4): "(A) No person shall knowingly make a false statement, or knowingly swear or affirm the truth of a false statement previously made, when any of the following apply. . . . (4) the statement is made with purpose to secure the payment of workman's compensation, unemployment compensation, aid for the aged, aid for the blind, aid for the permanently and totally disabled, aid to dependent children, general relief, retirement benefits, or other benefits administered by a governmental agency or paid out of a public treasury." The state criminal code distinguishes criminal acts as first, second, third, or fourth degree, according to perceived seriousness. Penalties, then, vary not only by felony and misdemeanor, but by degree.

25. For an explanation, see chapter 3.

26. Ohio Revised Code, section 2951.02(B) (9); (C).

27. Ohio Department of Public Welfare, *Medicaid Provider Handbook* (1977), section 106.2–106.21.

28. "Revco Convicted of Using False Billings to Collect on Ohio Medicaid Prescriptions," *Wall Street Journal,* 1 August 1977.

29. Organizational Criminal Liability, Ohio Revised Code 2901.33(A) (4) states an organization may be convicted of an offense under several circumstances, one of which is

> If acting with the kind of culpability otherwise required for the commission of the offense, its commission was authorized, requested, commanded, tolerated, or performed by the board of directors, trustees, partners, or by a high managerial officer, agent or employee acting in behalf of the organization and within the scope of his office or employment.

30. This amount was confirmed in Ohio Department of Public Welfare, Division of Medical Assistance, Bureau of Surveillance and Utilization Review, *Final Report of Examination of Provider Records,* 24 July 1977.

31. Personal Accountability for Organizational Conduct, Ohio Revised Code 2901.24:

> An officer, agent or employee of an organization . . . may be prosecuted for an offense committed by such organization, if he acts with the kind of culpability required for the commission of the offense, and. . . . (1) in the name of the organization or in its

behalf, he engages in conduct constituting the offense, or causes another to engage in such conduct, or tolerates such conduct when it is of a type for which he has direct responsibility.

32. *Columbus Dispatch,* 28 July 1977, and *Wall Street Journal,* 1 August 1977.

33. Correspondence, Revco Drug Stores, Inc., to Ohio Department of Public Welfare, 24 October 1977.

34. Entry, Case No. 80 EX-06-48, Court of Common Pleas, Franklin County, Ohio, Criminal Division, 1 April 1981.

35. Memorandum, James W. Lewis, attorney, Columbus, Ohio, September 1981.

CHAPTER 2

1. Mayer N. Zald, "On the Social Control of Industries," *Social Forces* 57 (September 1978): 85. There are a few empirical studies, however: see Robert N. Stern, "The Development of an Interorganizational Control Network: The Case of Intercollegiate Athletics," *Administrative Science Quarterly* 24 (June 1979): 242–266; Michel Crozier and Jean-Claude Thoenig, "The Regulation of Complex Organized Systems," *Administrative Science Quarterly* 21 (December 1976): 547–570.

2. Phillip Selznick, *The Organizational Weapon* (Glencoe: Free Press, 1960), Introduction.

3. Ibid.

4. Rita Braito, Steve Paulson, and Gerald Klonglon, "Domain Consensus: A Key Variable in Interorganizational Analysis," in Marlin B. Brinkerhoff and Phillip R. Kunz, eds., *Complex Organizations and Their Environments* (Dubuque: William C. Brown, 1972), pp. 176–192.

5. Ibid., p. 180. See also Brian C. Aldrich, "Relations between Organizations: A Critical Review of the Literature" (University of Minnesota, 1970, mimeographed).

6. See Thomas R. Forrest, "Emergent Organization: A New Approach for Study" (M.A. thesis, Ohio State University, 1968), and *Structural Differentiation in Emergent Groups* (Columbus: Disaster Research Center, Ohio State University, 1974).

7. James N. Rosenau, "Toward the Study of National-International Linkages," in James N. Rosenau, ed., *Linkage Politics: Essays on the Consequences of National and International Systems* (New York: Free Press, 1969), pp. 44–63; Adrian F. Aveni, "Organizational Linkages and Resource Mobilization: The Significance of Linkage Strength and Breadth," *Sociological Quarterly* 19 (1978): 185–202.

8. James D. Thompson, *Organizations in Action* (New York: McGraw-Hill, 1967), p. 29.

9. The definition of organizational resources is from Howard E. Aldrich, "Organizational Boundaries and Interorganizational Conflict," *Human Relations* 24 (1971): 284. I have added organizational sanctions.

10. Aiken and Hage point out that social service organizations have only limited opportunity for incremental state assistance, and so a major way they increase resources is through joint programs with other organizations in the same field. A joint program, however, differs from a network in that the former is often a relatively enduring relationship, thus indicating a high degree of organizational interdependence. Despite this distinction, the limited opportunity to obtain additional resources from the state is also relevant to the social control network's formation. Michael Aiken and Jerald Hage, "Organizational Interdependence and Intraorganizational Structure," *American Sociological Review* 33 (1968): 912–930.

11. Joseph E. Wright, "Interorganizational Systems and Networks in Mass Casualty Situations" (Ph.D. dissertation, Ohio State University, 1976). Some might suggest the term "coalition," which frequently has been used to describe organizations coming together on an ad hoc basis when common organizational goals coincide (Roland Warren, "The Interorganizational Field as a Focus of Investigation," *Administrative Science Quarterly* 12 [December 1967]: 396–419), or the term "action set," which refers to a group of organizations formed into a temporary alliance for a limited purpose (Howard E. Aldrich, *Organizations and Environments* [Englewood Cliffs: Prentice-Hall, 1979], pp. 280–281, 316–321). However, because Wright's model theoretically specifies and empirically substantiates not only how these organizations come together, but also patterns of relationships between units, his concept of focused network more accurately describes this case.

12. Wright, p. 12.

13. Among the seven organizations, linkages between state agencies were common, whereas linkages between the county and state organizations were not as common. The state organizations each had established linkages with an average of five of the other organizations. The single county organization, the Economic Crime Unit, had established linkages with only two of the other relevant organizations prior to the Revco case. See table 1.

14. Sol Levine and Paul E. White, "Exchange as a Conceptual Framework for the Study of Interorganizational Relationships," in Brinkerhoff and Kunz, p. 355. See also Aveni, pp. 185–202; Jeffrey Pfeffer and Gerald R. Salancik, *The External Control of Organizations: A Resource Dependence Perspective* (New York: Harper and Row, 1978), p. 221.

15. For greater detail on the selection process for each primary and peripheral organization, see Vaughan, "Crime between Organizations," chapter 2.

16. Wright, p. 17.

17. Ibid.

18. Howard E. Aldrich and David A. Whetten, "Organization Sets, Action Sets and Networks: Making the Most of Simplicity," in Paul C. Nystrom and William H. Starbuck, eds., *Handbook of Organizational Design*, vol. 1 (New York: Oxford University Press, 1981), pp. 385–408.

19. See Karl E. Weick, "Educational Organizations as Loosely Coupled Systems," *Administrative Science Quarterly* 21 (March 1976): 1–19; Ronald G. Corwin, "Organizations as Loosely Coupled Systems: Evolution of a Perspective" (Paper presented at seminar, Educational Organizations as Loosely Coupled Systems, Palo Alto, California, November 13–14, 1976); and Alvin Gouldner, "Reciprocity and Autonomy in Functional Theory," in Llewellyn Gross, ed., *Symposium on Sociological Theory* (New York: Harper and Row, 1960), pp. 241–270.

20. Corwin, p. 1.

21. Wright, p. 12.

22. See details in chapter 3.

23. Interviews: Ohio Department of Public Welfare, 11 January 1978; Ohio State Highway Patrol, 17 July 1978; Ohio State Board of Pharmacy, 27 July 1978.

24. Eugene Litwak and Lydia Hylton, "Interorganizational Analysis: An Hypothesis on Coordinating Agencies," *Administrative Science Quarterly* 10 (1962): 395–420.

25. See also Howard Guetzkow, "Relations among Organizations," in Raymond Bowers, ed., *Studies of Behavior in Organizations* (Athens: University of Georgia Press, 1966), p. 38.

26. William Graham Sumner, *Folkways: A Study of the Sociological Importance of Usages, Manners, Customs, Mores, and Morals* (Boston: Ginn and Co., 1906).

27. I am indebted to Geoffrey Webster, attorney-at-law, Columbus, Ohio, for this insight.

28. Arthur L. Stinchcombe, "Social Structure and Organizations," in James G. March, ed., *Handbook of Organizations* (Chicago: Rand McNally, 1965), pp. 146–160.

29. Stinchcombe, pp. 149–150.

30. "Revco Medicaid Overbilling Settlement Hit by Ferguson," *Columbus Dispatch*, 5 August 1977; Interviews, Ohio State Office of Attorney General, 24 April 1978.

31. The mechanism the attorney general's office used for bringing suit on behalf of the state was the federal False Claims Act of 1863. This Civil War statute was created to regulate attempts to defraud the United States or any agents thereof of its money. The act delegates authority for enforcement to the Justice Department, United States attorney, or United States district attorney. In the event these agents decline to pros-

ecute, any citizen in the state could initiate civil suit in his own behalf as a private citizen. The state attorney general, acting as a private citizen, can file suits for defrauding the United States in federal courts (31 USCA 232).

32. The new bill stated:

> (B) When it appears to the Attorney General, as a result of an investigation under (A) of this section, that there is a cause to prosecute for the commission of a crime or to pursue a civil remedy, he may refer the evidence to the Prosecuting Attorney having jurisdiction of the matter, or to a regular grand jury drawn and impaneled pursuant to sections 2939.01 to 2939.24 of the Revised Code, or to a special grand jury drawn and impaneled pursuant to section 2939.17 of the Revised Code, or *he may initiate and prosecute any necessary criminal or civil actions* in this state. When proceeding under this section, the Attorney General and any assistant or special counsel designated by him for that purpose, has all rights, privileges, and powers of prosecuting attorneys. The Attorney General shall have exclusive supervision and control of all investigations and prosecutions initiated by him under this section. Nothing in this section shall prevent a Prosecuting Attorney from investigating and prosecuting criminal activity related to Chapter 3721 and Section 5101.51 of the Revised Code. ([Emphasis added] Ohio S.B. No. 159, signed into law 24 April 1978).

33. Public Law 95-142, 91 STAT. 1175, 95th Congress, 25 October 1977.

34. Stern notes the importance of supraordinate systems in influencing network structure. See "The Development of an Interorganizational Control Network."

35. Georg Simmel, *Conflict and the Web of Group Affiliations,* translated by Kurt H. Wolff and Reinhard Bendix (New York: Free Press, 1956), pp. 98–102.

36. See John R. Kimberly et al., *The Organizational Life Cycle: Issues in the Creation, Transformation, and Decline of Organizations* (San Francisco: Jossey-Bass, 1980).

37. Simmel, pp. 98–102.

38. Michael Hannan and John Freeman, "The Population Ecology of Organizations," *American Journal of Sociology* 82 (1977): 929–964; Paul J. DiMaggio and Walter W. Powell, "The Iron Cage Revisited: Institutional Isomorphism and Collective Rationality in Organizational Fields," *American Sociological Review* (forthcoming 1983).

39. See Robert K. Merton, *Social Theory and Social Structure* (New York: Free Press, 1968).

40. Merton, pp. 86–90.

41. See, for example, Richard H. Hall, "Professionalism and Bureaucratization," *American Sociological Review* 33 (February 1968): 92–104.

42. The insularity problem and its explanation emerged during a meeting with representatives of the Office of Inspector General and the Office of Quality Control, Department of Health, Education, and Welfare, Washington, D.C., November 1979. The responsibility of those attending was surveillance, prevention, and control of Medicaid fraud and abuse. For a discussion of the prospects and problems of agency cooperation between federal, state, and local levels, see Norman Abrahms, "Assessing the Federal Government's 'War' on White Collar Crime," *Temple Law Quarterly* 53 (1980): 984–1008.

43. While this book focuses on large complex organizations, the vast majority of organizations in the United States are quite small. See Aldrich, *Organizations and Environments,* pp. 40–44.

CHAPTER 3

1. "Revco Fined, Returns Welfare Cash," *Columbus Citizen-Journal,* 10 July 1977.

2. Interviews: Ohio Department of Public Welfare, 11 January 1978; Ohio State Highway Patrol, 17 July 1978; Ohio State Board of Pharmacy, 27 July 1978.

3. "Revco Medicaid Overbilling Settlement Hit by Ferguson," *Columbus Dispatch,* 5 August 1977; Interviews, Ohio State Office of Attorney General, 24 April 1978.

4. See, for example, Phillip Selznick, *TVA and the Grass Roots* (Berkeley: University of California Press, 1949).

5. My thanks to an anonymous reviewer for this point.

6. Lawrence W. Sherman, "Three Models of Organizational Corruption in Agencies of Social Control," *Social Problems* 27 (April 1980): 478–491.

7. Sherman, p. 483.

8. Material sanctions are those relied upon by the legal system, such as incarceration and fines. Though extralegal systems of social control may also rely on material sanctions, they more frequently employ sanctions directed at the symbolic aspects of deviant actors: their reputations, status, trustworthiness. See Lawrence W. Sherman, *Scandal and Reform: Controlling Police Corruption* (Berkeley: University of California Press, 1978), pp. 24–26.

9. Ohio Revised Code, sections 2923.04, 2913.42, 2913.02 (A) (3), 2921.13 (A) (4).

10. State versus Schneider, Case No. 77AP-662 (1977 Decisions, p. 4914), unreported decision of Franklin County Court of Appeals. At this writing, a bill is under consideration in the Ohio legislature which

145

would remedy the penalty structure for cases with large amounts of loss.

11. Ohio Revised Code, section 2951.02 (B) (9), (C).

12. Interviews, Economic Crime Unit, 1 June 1978, 10 June 1978.

13. "Revco Convicted of Using False Billings to Collect on Ohio Medicaid Prescriptions," *Wall Street Journal,* 1 August 1977.

14. Peter M. Blau and W. Richard Scott, *Formal Organizations* (San Francisco: Chandler, 1962).

15. For a discussion of the link between publicity and the symbolic sanctioning of organizational deviance, see Lawrence W. Sherman, "The Mobilization of Scandal," in *Scandal and Reform,* pp. 59–91.

16. For the sociologist some of these indicators were easily interpretable. Others were not. For this reason the discussion of impact of investigation and sanctions on Revco is based on an analysis done in collaboration with a certified financial analyst, see Oberg, pp. 190–200.

17. Revco Drug Stores, Inc., Annual Report, Fiscal Year Ended 28 May 1977, Twinsburg, Ohio.

18. Oberg, p. 193.

19. The three selected were Eckerd, Gray, and Rite Aid drug stores, which were chosen because of their similarity to Revco in terms of sales trends, store expansion, magnitude of earnings, and pricing policies.

20. Oberg, p. 190.

21. Ibid., pp. 190–192.

22. All newspaper articles related to the case were used in this analysis. *Columbus Dispatch, Columbus Citizen-Journal, Cleveland Plain Dealer, Cincinnati Enquirer,* and *Wall Street Journal* were the sources.

23. Oberg, p. 192.

24. Ibid., pp. 193–194.

25. Ibid., p. 196.

26. Revco Drug Stores, Inc., Third Quarter Report, March 1978.

CHAPTER 4

1. The importance of studying not only the organization, but the environment in which organizations exist is an established tradition among organizational sociologists. See, for example, William M. Evan, "The Organization-Set: Toward a Theory of Interorganizational Relations," in James D. Thompson, ed., *Approaches to Organizational Design* (Pittsburgh: University of Pittsburgh Press, 1966), pp. 173–191; F. E. Emery and E. L. Trist, "The Causal Texture of Organizational Environments," *Human Relations* 18 (1965): 21–32; Aldrich, *Organizations and Environments;* Pfeffer and Salancik, *The External Control of Organizations.* For an analysis of how this trend has influenced the research of sociologists interested in deviance and social control, see Diane Vaughan, "Recent

Developments in White-Collar Crime Theory and Research," in Israel L. Barak-Glantz and C. Ronald Huff, eds., *The Mad, the Bad, and the Different: Essays in Honor of Simon Dinitz* (Lexington, Mass.: Lexington Books, 1981), pp. 135–147.

2. Robert K. Merton, "Social Structure and Anomie," in *Social Theory and Social Structure*, pp. 185–214. Stinchcombe points out that Merton distinguishes between the structural sources of motivation (cultural structure) and the structuring of alternatives (social structure) in order to separate the motivational aspect of the structured alternatives from the goals people are trying to reach by choosing these alternatives. The two interact: motivation and constraints on alternatives produce differential rates of choice of alternatives. Arthur L. Stinchcombe, "Merton's Theory of Social Structure," in Lewis A. Coser, ed., *The Idea of Social Structure: Papers in Honor of Robert K. Merton* (New York: Harcourt Brace Jovanovich, 1975), pp. 18–20. For a critique of this distinction see Edwin M. Lemert, "Social Structure, Social Control, and Deviation," in Marshall B. Clinard, ed., *Anomie and Deviant Behavior: A Discussion and Critique* (New York: Free Press, 1964), pp. 57–97.

3. Merton, "Social Structure and Anomie," p. 195.

4. Merton gives no citations for research or official statistics supporting this conclusion. Interestingly, he discusses the extent of "white-collar crime" for three pages and cites five sources which reinforce the fact that crime by other social classes is a frequent and underestimated phenomenon. Ibid., pp. 195–198.

5. Ibid., pp. 194–195. In later writings, Merton emphasized that pecuniary success is one dominant theme in American culture, and that the extreme emphasis on any goal, any achievement, without equal emphasis on institutionally legitimate means for attainment will create a strain toward deviance. He selects the goal of monetary success as illustrative because in American society it has become so widely accepted that it has become a cultural doctrine—a socially defined expectation, regarded as appropriate for everyone, irrespective of station in life. See "Social Structure and Anomie: Continuities," in *Social Theory and Social Structure* pp. 220–221.

6. Lemert, pp. 62–66.

7. See, for example, John C. Coffee, Jr., "'No Soul to Damn, No Body to Kick': An Unscandalized Inquiry into the Problem of Corporate Punishment," *Michigan Law Review* 79 (January 1981): 395; Milton Friedman, *Capitalism and Freedom* (Chicago: University of Chicago Press, 1962), p. 133, and "The Social Responsibility of Business Is to Increase Its Profits," *New York Times*, 12 September 1962, p. 126.

8. F. M. Scherer, *Industrial Market Structure and Economic Performance*, 2d ed. (Chicago: Rand McNally, 1980), pp. 29–37.

9. David R. Kamerschen, "The Economic Effects of Monopoly: A Lawyer's Guide to Antitrust Economics," in Terry Calvani and John Siegfried, eds., *Economic Analysis and Antitrust Law* (Boston: Little, Brown, 1979), pp. 28–32.

10. James G. March and Herbert A. Simon, *Organizations* (New York: John Wiley and Sons, 1958), pp. 113–117, 138–142, 169–171.

11. Scherer, p. 38.

12. Merton, "Social Structure and Anomie," p. 188.

13. Lemert, p. 59.

14. Cloward and Ohlin support this interpretation. See Richard A. Cloward and Lloyd E. Ohlin, *Delinquency and Opportunity: A Theory of Delinquent Gangs* (New York: Free Press, 1960), p. 83.

15. Yuchtman and Seashore describe the competition among organizations for scarce and valued resources as

> a continuous process underlying the emergence of a universal hierarchical differentiation among social organizations. Such a hierarchy is an excellent yardstick against which to assess organizational effectiveness. It reflects what may be referred to as the 'bargaining position' of the organization in relation to resources and in relation to competing social entities that share all or part of the organizational environment.

See Ephraim Yuchtman and Stanley E. Seashore, "A System Resource Approach to Organizational Effectiveness," *American Sociological Review* 32 (1967): 897–898. Aldrich also treats the environment as consisting of resources for which organizations compete, with the levels of resources and the terms under which they are made available as critical. See Aldrich, *Organizations and Environments*, pp. 61–70.

16. Pfeffer and Salancik, pp. 39–59. A. O. Hirschman, *Exit, Voice, and Loyalty* (Cambridge: Harvard University Press, 1970), pp. 4, 21–54.

17. For a thorough discussion of barriers to entry that prevent potential entrants from gaining a position in a market, see Aldrich, *Organizations and Environments*, pp. 149–153, 184–187.

18. Staw and Szwajkowski's research tests the hypothesis that the more scarce the environment of a business organization, the more likely it will engage in illegal acts in order to procure additional resources. They found that environmental scarcity does appear to be related to a range of violations. See Barry M. Staw and Eugene Szwajkowski, "The Scarcity Munificence Component of Organizational Environments and the Commission of Illegal Acts," *Administrative Science Quarterly* 20 (1975): 345–354.

19. Cloward and Ohlin's ideas on standards for individual success are the basis for these organizational standards. Cloward and Ohlin, p. 94.

20. For discussions of how the environment can affect goal-setting in organizations, see James Thompson and William McEwen, "Organizational Goals and Environment: Goal-setting as an Interaction Process," *American Sociological Review* 23 (1958): 23–31; and John K. Maniha and Charles Perrow, "The Reluctant Organization and the Aggressive Environment," *Administrative Science Quarterly* 10 (1965): 238–257.

21. Arthur L. Stinchcombe, "Social Structure and Organizations," pp. 142–193, especially pp. 169–180.

22. Ibid., p. 174.

23. Ibid.

24. Ibid., p. 175.

25. Gilbert Geis, "The Heavy Electrical Equipment Antitrust Cases of 1961," in Marshall B. Clinard and Richard Quinney, eds., *Criminal Behavior Systems* (New York: Holt, Rinehart and Winston, 1967), pp. 139–151; Edward Gross, "Organizational Crime: A Theoretical Perspective," in Norman Denzin, ed., *Studies in Symbolic Interaction*, vol. 1 (Greenwich, Conn.: JAI Press), pp. 55–85; Ronald C. Kramer, "Corporate Crime: An Organizational Perspective" (Paper presented at the Conference on White-Collar and Economic Crime, Potsdam, New York, 7–9 February 1980).

26. Merton, "Social Structure and Anomie," p. 195.

27. Robert K. Merton, "Anomie, Anomia, and Social Interaction: Contexts of Deviant Behavior," in Clinard, p. 235.

28. Merton, "Anomie, Anomia, and Social Interaction," p. 235. Also see Stinchcombe, "Merton's Theory of Social Structure," pp. 23–24.

29. Lemert, p. 69.

30. Merton, "Anomie, Anomia, and Social Interaction," p. 235; Stinchcombe, "Merton's Theory of Social Structure," pp. 23–24.

31. K. Levine, "Empiricism in Victimological Research: A Critique," *Victimology: An International Journal* 3 (1978): 88.

32. Cloward and Ohlin, p. 94.

33. For examples, see Susan P. Shapiro, "Detecting Illegalities: A Perspective on the Control of Securities Violations" (Ph.D. dissertation, Yale University, 1980), p. 259.

34. Richard A. Cloward, "Illegitimate Means, Anomie, and Deviant Behavior," *American Sociological Review* 24 (April 1959): 164–176.

35. I am indebted to Frederick H. Decker for this observation.

36. Sherman, "Three Models of Organizational Corruption," p. 478.

37. Scherer, pp. 29–37; for a discussion of the methodologically based controversy on the diverse goals of organizations, see Charles

Perrow, "The Analysis of Goals in Complex Organizations," *American Sociological Review* 26 (December 1961): 859–866, and Hall, pp. 94–96.

38. Christopher D. Stone, *Where the Law Ends: The Social Control of Corporate Behavior* (New York: Harper and Row, 1975); Staw and Szwajkowski, pp. 345–354; Gross, "Organizational Crime"; Kramer.

39. See, for example, Donald R. Cressey, *Other People's Money: A Study in the Social Psychology of Embezzlement* (Glencoe: Free Press, 1953).

40. See Lemert, p. 62, for a similar viewpoint.

41. Merton, "Continuities," p. 226.

42. Lemert, p. 68; Clinard, p. 43. However, Ewick states, "The fact that deviance fails to occur under these conditions (and occurs when they are absent) merely suggests that structural strain is not a necessary and sufficient cause of deviance. To deny the relation between deviance and anomie on these grounds would be like arguing that hunger is not causally related to eating because people sometimes eat when they are not [hungry] and refrain from eating when they are" (Patricia M. Ewick, memorandum, February 1981).

CHAPTER 5

1. Cloward, pp. 164–176. Also see Cloward and Ohlin.

2. See, for example, Edward Gross, "Organization Structure and Organizational Crime," in Gilbert Geis and Ezra Stotland, eds., *White-Collar Crime: Theory and Research,* Sage Criminal Justice System Annuals, vol. 13 (Beverly Hills: Sage Publications, 1980), pp. 52–76; and Stone.

3. See, for example, Jacob Perez, "Corporate Criminality: A Study of the One-Thousand Largest Industrial Corporations in the U.S.A." (Ph.D. dissertation, University of Pennsylvania, 1978); and Marshall B. Clinard and Peter C. Yeager, *Corporate Crime* (New York: Free Press, 1980).

4. Peter Asch and J. J. Seneca, "Is Collusion Profitable?" *Review of Economics and Statistics* 58 (February 1976): 1–12; Perez; Marshall B. Clinard et al., *Illegal Corporate Behavior* (Washington, D.C.: Department of Justice, Law Enforcement Assistance Administration, National Institute of Law Enforcement and Criminal Justice, 1979).

5. Hall also suggests that complexity may be more important than the size factor in understanding organizations. Richard H. Hall, *Organizations: Structure and Process* (Englewood Cliffs: Prentice-Hall, 1972), p. 171.

6. James S. Coleman, "Legitimate and Illegitimate Use of Power," in Coser, pp. 234–235.

7. Selznick, *The Organizational Weapon,* p. 36.

8. Diane Rothbard Margolis, *The Managers: Corporate Life in America* (New York: Morrow, 1979), pp. 41–66, 93–116.

9. Stinchcombe, "Social Structure and Organizations," pp. 142–193, especially pp. 169–180.

10. Stinchcombe, "Merton's Theory of Social Structure," pp. 17–23; Lemert, pp. 70–75.

11. Aldrich explains this variability as "active loose coupling," which occurs when a subunit of an organization is more tightly coupled to an environmental sector than other subunits, and a feedback loop connects environmental conditions with organizational responses:

> A feedback loop is present when an organizational mechanism for monitoring the environment exists, and when the state of the environment (or intended target of the organization's action) is compared to some desired state by members of the organization. The feedback loop is closed when members of the organization take action to move the organization to the desired position vis-à-vis the environment, and the results of their actions are monitored and compared to the condition. The cycle repeats until the desired state is achieved, whether it be one of selling a million toothbrushes or converting a million souls.

See Aldrich, *Organizations and Environments,* pp. 84–85.

12. Lemert, pp. 62–71.

13. Ibid., pp. 70–73; Stinchcombe, "Merton's Theory of Social Structure," p. 17.

14. Lemert, p. 63.

15. Stinchcombe, "Merton's Theory of Social Structure," p. 21.

16. Peter M. Blau, *Exchange and Power in Social Life* (New York: John Wiley and Sons, 1964), pp. 119–125, 140–142.

17. Coffee reports a case of intraorganizational competition where "two wholly owned subsidiaries of U.S. Steel . . . have been actively lobbying with regard to proposed legislation, *but on opposite sides*" (emphasis in original). John C. Coffee, Jr., "Beyond the Shut-Eyed Sentry: Toward a Theoretical View of Corporate Misconduct and an Effective Legal Response," *Virginia Law Review* 63 (1977): 1035.

18. See Perrow, pp. 859–866; and Oliver Williamson, *Corporate Control and Business Behavior: An Inquiry into the Effects of Organization Form on Enterprise Behavior* (Englewood Cliffs: Prentice-Hall, 1970), as quoted in Coffee, "Beyond the Shut-Eyed Sentry," p. 1135.

19. J. Patrick Wright, *On A Clear Day You Can See General Motors* (Grosse Pointe, Michigan: Wright Enterprises, 1979), pp. 73–97.

20. Technology is used here as described by Hickson et al.: operations technology, materials technology, and knowledge technology.

D. J. Hickson, D. S. Pugh, and Diana C. Pheysey, "Operations Technology and Organizational Structure: An Empirical Reappraisal," *Administrative Science Quarterly* 14 (September 1969): 378–397, as cited in Hall, *Organizations,* p. 181.

21. See Daniel Nelson, *Managers and Workers: Origins of the New Factory System in the United States, 1880–1920* (Madison: University of Wisconsin Press, 1975), for a discussion of the development of task segregation in organizations as a protective device against high personnel turnover.

22. Hall, *Organizations,* pp. 173, 196.

23. See Gouldner, pp. 241–270; and Weick, pp. 1–19.

24. Gordon Tullock, *The Politics of Bureaucracy* (Washington, D.C.: Public Affairs Press, 1964), as cited in Coffee, "Beyond the Shut-Eyed Sentry," pp. 1136–1137.

25. See James C. Emery, *Organizational Planning and Control Systems* (New York: Macmillan, 1969); also Louis Kriesberg, "Note: Decision-Making Models and the Control of Corporate Crime," *Yale Law Journal* 85 (1976): 1091, as cited in Coffee, "Beyond the Shut-Eyed Sentry," p. 1101.

26. Coffee, "Beyond the Shut-Eyed Sentry," pp. 1134–1147.

27. John E. Conklin, *Illegal but Not Criminal: Business Crime in America* (Englewood Cliffs: Prentice-Hall, 1977), p. 65.

28. See chapter 1. For an extended discussion of how this organizational characteristic relates to legal issues of responsibility for organizational behavior, see Stone, pp. 60–69.

29. Coffee, "Beyond the Shut-Eyed Sentry," p. 1127.

30. Donald R. Cressey and Charles A. Moore, *Corporation Codes of Ethical Conduct: Report to the Peat, Marwick, and Mitchell Foundation* (New York: Peat, Marwick, and Mitchell, 1980), p. 85.

31. James E. Sorensen, Hugh D. Grove, and Thomas L. Sorensen, "Detecting Management Fraud: The Role of the Independent Auditor," in Geis and Stotland, p. 235.

32. Michael Spence, *Market Signaling* (Cambridge: Harvard University Press, 1974).

33. Ibid., pp. 6–9.

34. Ibid., pp. 9–11.

35. Ibid.

36. Ibid., p. 10.

37. Lange and Bowers, p. 24.

38. Ibid., pp. 25, 26.

39. Ibid., p. 25.

40. M. G. Wiley and M. N. Zald, "The Growth and Transformation of Educational Accrediting Agencies: An Exploratory Study of the Social Control of Institutions," *Sociology of Education* 41 (1968): 35–56. Kermit

Vandiver, "Why Should My Conscience Bother Me?" in M. David Ermann and Richard J. Lundman, eds., *Corporate and Governmental Deviance: Problems of Organizational Behavior in Contemporary Society* (New York: Oxford University Press, 1978), pp. 80–101.

41. Russell R. Dynes and E. L. Quarantelli, "Organizations as Victims in Mass Civil Disturbances," in Israel Drapkin and Emilio Viano, eds., *Victimology: A New Focus,* vol. 5 (Lexington, Massachusetts: D. C. Heath, 1974), pp. 67–77.

42. Ibid., p. 71.

43. Ibid., p. 72.

44. Donald R. Cressey, *Other People's Money* (Glencoe: Free Press, 1953), pp. 81–82.

45. Merton, "Social Structure and Anomie," pp. 185–214; Cloward and Ohlin.

46. Cloward, p. 168; Cloward and Ohlin, pp. 124–129, 148.

47. Cloward, p. 173.

48. Merton, "Social Structure and Anomie."

CHAPTER 6

1. Pfeffer and Salancik, pp. 40–54.

2. "Safety Group Links 36 Deaths in Fires to Certain Toyotas," *Wall Street Journal,* 17 November 1980, p. 7.

3. Jack Katz, "Cover-Up and Collective Integrity: On the Natural Antagonisms of Authority Internal and External to Organizations," *Social Problems* 25 (1979): 3–17.

4. For an extended discussion of the positive and negative ramifications of organizational secrets, see *Society* 16, no. 4 (May–June 1979), especially Patricia E. Erickson et al., "Organizational Secrecy and Environmental Control," pp. 46–51; Stanton F. Tefft, "The Politics of Secrecy," pp. 60–67; Brian J. O'Connell, "Secrecy in Business," pp. 40–45.

5. Stone, pp. 93–110.

6. Pfeffer and Salancik, p. 41.

7. Ibid.

8. Ibid.

9. Aldrich, *Organizations and Environments,* p. 266.

10. Peter M. Gerhart, *Report on the Empirical Case Studies Project to the National Commission for the Review of Antitrust Laws and Procedures,* vol. 2 (Washington, D.C.: United States Government Printing Office, 1979).

11. Pfeffer and Salancik, p. 216.

12. Neal Shover, "The Criminalization of Corporate Behavior: Federal Surface Coal Mining," in Geis and Stotland, pp. 98–125.

13. Ibid., p. 124.

14. Pfeffer and Salancik, p. 214.

15. George Katona, *Price Control and Business* (Bloomington: Principia Press, 1945); Staw and Szwajkowski, pp. 345–354; Clinard et al.

16. Pfeffer and Salancik, p. 220.

17. Stone, p. 124.

18. Conklin, pp. 122, 124; Pfeffer and Salancik, pp. 161–165.

19. Stone, p. 95; Conklin, p. 122–123.

20. Stone, p. 109.

21. For a discussion of law enforcement's need for a reliable information base on which to act, see Mark Richard, "Introduction: Symposium on White-Collar Crime," *Temple Law Quarterly* 53 (1980): 976–980.

22. Stone, pp. 106–110; Pfeffer and Salancik, pp. 210–211.

23. Pfeffer and Salancik, p. 210.

24. Stone, p. 96.

25. Kenneth Mann, "Defending White-Collar Crime" (Ph.D. dissertation, Yale University, 1980).

26. John Hagan, Ilene H. (Bernstein) Nagel, and Celesta Albonetti, "The Differential Sentencing of White-Collar Offenders in Ten Federal District Courts," *American Sociological Review* 45 (October 1980): 802–820; and Sherman, "Three Models of Organizational Corruption," pp. 478–491.

27. Peter M. Gerhart, "Corporate Giantism and Effective Antitrust Enforcement" (Paper presented at American Society of Criminology Annual Meetings, Philadelphia, Pennsylvania, 7–9 November 1980), p. 5.

28. Pfeffer and Salancik, p. 221.

29. Among the noteworthy are the establishment of the Environmental Protection Agency in 1970 and the amendments passed in 1972 to the Federal Water Pollution Control Act of 1948. See Peter C. Yeager and Marshall B. Clinard, "Regulating Corporate Behavior: A Case Study," in Paul Brantingham and Jack Kress, eds., *Structure, Law, and Power: Essays in the Sociology of Law* (Beverly Hills: Sage Publications, 1979), chapter 4.

30. Pfeffer and Salancik, p. 141.

31. Evan, pp. 173–191; Pfeffer and Salancik.

32. G. J. Stigler, "The Theory of Economic Regulation," *Bell Journal of Economics and Management Science* 2 (1971): 3–21, in Pfeffer and Salancik, pp. 204–206.

33. Pfeffer and Salancik, p. 51.

34. Gerald R. Salancik, "The Role of Interdependence in Organizational Responsiveness to Demands from the Environment: The Case

of Women versus Power" (University of Illinois, 1976, Mimeographed), as cited in Pfeffer and Salancik, pp. 56–59.

35. Patricia M. Ewick, *Theories of Organizational Illegality: A Reconceptualization*, Yale Working Paper series, vol. 2 (New Haven: Department of Sociology, 1981), p. 19.

36. Wiley and Zald, pp. 36–56.

CHAPTER 7

1. See, for example, Conklin; Stone; and Clinard et al.

2. Conklin; Clinard et al.; Gilbert Geis, "Deterring Corporate Crime," in Ralph Nader and Mark J. Green, eds., *Corporate Power in America* (New York: Viking, 1973), pp. 246–258; Stone; Vaughan, "Crime between Organizations"; Ralph Nader, Mark Green, and Joel Seligman, *Taming the Giant Corporation* (New York: Norton, 1976).

3. Vaughan, "Crime between Organizations"; Nader, Green, and Seligman; Stone; M. David Ermann and Richard J. Lundman, "Deviant Acts by Complex Organizations: Deviance and Social Control at the Organizational Level of Analysis," *Sociological Quarterly* 19 (1978): 55–65.

4. See also Gary T. Marx, "Ironies of Social Control: Authorities as Contributors to Deviance through Escalation, Nonenforcement, and Covert Facilitation," *Social Problems* 28 (1981): 222–246.

5. Ewick, p. 12.

6. Albert K. Cohen, *Deviance and Control* (Englewood Cliffs: Prentice-Hall, 1966), p. 6; Hall, *Organizations*, pp. 173–177.

7. Cohen, pp. 16–21.

8. Gross, "Organizational Crime," p. 63.

9. Zald, "On the Social Control of Industries," p. 85.

10. Albert D. Biderman and Albert J. Reiss, Jr., *Definitions and Criteria for a Selection of Prospective Federal Sources of White-Collar Crime Data*, Report No. 1, Grant No. 78-NI-AX-0132 (Washington, D.C.: Department of Justice, Law Enforcement Assistance Administration, National Institute of Law Enforcement and Criminal Justice, 1979), pp. 37–38.

11. C. P. Wolf, "The Accident at Three Mile Island: Social Science Perspectives," *Social Science Research Council Bulletin* 33 (1979): 58–59.

12. Edwin M. Schur, *Radical Nonintervention: Rethinking the Delinquency Problem* (Englewood Cliffs: Prentice-Hall, 1973).

13. Harold C. Barnett, "Corporate Capitalism, Corporate Crime" (Paper presented at Conference on White Collar and Economic Crime, State University of New York College at Postdam, 7–9 February 1980), pp. 13–14.

14. For suggestions addressing the other structural elements discussed, see especially Stone; Gross, "Organizational Crime"; and Martin L. Needleman and Carolyn Needleman, "Organizational Crime: Two Models of Criminogenesis," *Sociological Quarterly* 20 (1979): 517–528.

APPENDIX

1. Richard J. Lundman and Paul T. McFarlane, "Conflict Methodology: An Introduction and Preliminary Assessment," *Sociological Quarterly* 17 (1976): 503–512.

2. Rosalie H. Wax, "Gender and Age in Fieldwork and Fieldwork Education: No Good Thing Is Done by Any Man Alone," *Social Problems* 26 (1979): 509–522.

3. Geis, "Antitrust Cases of 1961," pp. 140–151.

4. For a general account of reasons why organizations resist research, see Chris Argyris, "Diagnosing Defenses against the Outsider," *Journal of Social Issues* 8 (1952): 24–34.

5. L. A. Dexter, *Elite and Specialized Interviewing* (Evanston: Northwestern University Press, 1970).

6. Morris S. Schwartz and Charlotte Green Schwartz, "Problems in Participant Observation," *American Journal of Sociology* 60 (1955): 343–354.

7. John Lofland, *Analyzing Social Settings* (Belmont, California: Wadsworth, 1971), pp. 73–133; Leonard Schatzman and Anselm L. Strauss, *Field Research: Strategies for a Natural Sociology* (Englewood Cliffs: Prentice-Hall, 1973), pp. 94–127.

8. Murray L. Wax, "Paradoxes of 'Consent' in the Practice of Fieldwork," *Social Problems* 27 (1980): 275.

9. John Van Maanen, "The Fact of Fiction in Organizational Ethnography," *Administrative Science Quarterly* 24 (1979): 539–550.

10. John Van Maanen, "Reclaiming Qualitative Methods for Organizational Research: A Preface," *Administrative Science Quarterly* 24 (1979): 522; see also Andrew M. Pettigrew, "On Studying Organizational Cultures," *Administrative Science Quarterly* 24 (1979): 570–581.

11. William F. Whyte, *Street Corner Society* (Chicago: University of Chicago Press, 1955; 3d ed., revised and expanded, 1981).

12. Oberg, pp. 190–200.

13. This was one of the circumstances mentioned earlier which called for renegotiation of consent.

14. For an exposition of the advantages and disadvantages of acceptance in the research setting, see Florence Kluckhohn, "The Participant Observer Technique in Small Communities," *American Journal of Sociology* 46 (1940): 331–343; and Schwartz and Schwartz.

15. Prior to the meeting, each individual had been given a copy of the final research results to review, to correct errors of fact, and to

critique for alternative interpretations. The confirmation of the written results contradicts the experience of Miles and his colleagues using a similar procedure (1979). Several possible factors may have influenced this outcome. Though the Revco research included eight organizations, only one event was studied (the investigation) which limited the research focus. Miles studied the evolution of six organizations over a four-year period: in other words, six events. This no doubt increased the number of interviewees, the volume of data, and the number of researchers necessary to do the work. The narrower scope of the Revco research made it possible for all the data to be stored in the experience, notes, files, and mind of one researcher. Discovery of factual error or discrepant observations did not depend upon transfer of data between researchers. Also, because all organizations participated in the same event, most of the information was confirmed by many sources both internal and external to the network. Whenever the information came from a single source, the organization from which it originated was identified in a footnote. Finally, in the Revco study the public setting for discussion of the final research results may have constrained attempts to "rewrite history" to make certain organizations appear in a more favorable light, although organization members had opportunities to discuss the results with me, privately. Miles and his colleagues apparently asked for written responses without providing a forum for their discussion, affording the subjects more privacy in which to air their opinions. See Matthew B. Miles, "Qualitative Data as an Attractive Nuisance: The Problem of Analysis," *Administrative Science Quarterly* 24 (1979): 591–601.

16. Carl Milofsky, "The Structure of Community Self-Help Organizations" (Paper presented at Midwestern Sociological Association, Milwaukee, Wisconsin. April 1980).

17. Howard S. Becker, "Whose Side Are We On?" *Social Problems* 14 (1967): 239–247.

18. The importance of analytically viewing the researcher's own use of language is stressed in Peter K. Manning, "Metaphors of the Field: Varieties of Organizational Discourse," *Administrative Science Quarterly* 24 (1979): 660–671.

19. Barney G. Glaser and Anselm L. Strauss, *The Discovery of Grounded Theory: Strategies for Qualitative Research* (Chicago: Aldine Publishing, 1967).

20. See Kluckhohn.

21. For related ideas concerning the role of peer support in separation processes, see Diane Vaughan, "Uncoupling: The Process of Moving from One Lifestyle to Another," *Alternative Lifestyles* 2 (1979): 415–442.

22. See also H. Kirk Downey and R. Duane Ireland, "Quantitative versus Qualitative: Environmental Assessment in Organizational Studies," *Administrative Science Quarterly* 24 (1979): 630–637.

23. Barney G. Glaser and Anselm L. Strauss, "The Discovery of Substantive Theory: A Basic Strategy Underlying Qualitative Research," *American Behavioral Scientist* 3 (February 1965): 5–12; Glaser and Strauss, *Grounded Theory.*

24. Glaser and Strauss, "Discovery of Substantive Theory," p. 8.

Selected Reading

Aiken, Michael, and Jerald Hage. "Organizational Interdependence and Intraorganizational Structure." *American Sociological Review* 33 (1968): 912–930.

Aldrich, Howard E. *Organizations and Environments.* Englewood Cliffs: Prentice-Hall, 1979.

———. "Resource Dependence and Interorganizational Relations." *Administration and Society* 7 (1976): 419–453.

Aldrich, Howard E., and Jeffrey Pfeffer. "Environments of Organizations." *Annual Review of Sociology* 2 (1976): 79–105.

Aldrich, Howard E., and David A. Whetten. "Organization Sets, Action Sets, and Networks: Making the Most of Simplicity." In *Handbook of Organizational Design,* vol. 1, edited by Paul Nystrom and William H. Starbuck, pp. 385–408. New York: Oxford University Press, 1981.

Anderson, Douglas D. "Who Owns the Regulators?" *Wharton Magazine* 4 (1980): 14–21.

Asch, Peter, and J. J. Seneca. "Is Collusion Profitable?" *Review of Economics and Statistics* 58 (1976): 1–12.

Aubert, Vilhelm. "White-Collar Crime and Social Structure." *American Journal of Sociology* 58 (1952): 263–271.

Aveni, Adrian F. "Organizational Linkages and Resource Mobilization: The Significance of Linkage Strength and Breadth." *Sociological Quarterly* 19 (1978): 185–202.

Bain, Joe S. *Barriers to New Competition.* Cambridge: Harvard University Press, 1956.

Banfield, Edward C. "Corruption as a Feature of Government Organization." *Journal of Law and Economics* 18 (1975): 587–606.

Barnett, Harold C. "Corporate Capitalism, Corporate Crime." *Crime and Delinquency* 27 (1981): 4–23.

Blau, Peter M. *Exchange and Power in Social Life.* New York: Wiley, 1964.

———, ed. *Approaches to the Study of Social Structure.* New York: Free Press, 1975.

Selected Reading

Braithwaite, John. "Inegalitarian Consequences of Egalitarian Reforms in the Control of Corporate Crime." *Temple Law Quarterly* 53 (1980): 1127–1146.
———. "The Limits of Economism in Controlling Harmful Corporate Conduct." *Law and Society Review* 16 (1981–1982): 481–504.
Brinkerhoff, Marlin B., and Phillip P. Kunz, eds. *Complex Organizations and Their Environments*. Dubuque: Brown, 1972.
Calvani, Terry, and John Siegfried, eds. *Economic Analysis and Antitrust Law*. Boston: Little, Brown, 1979.
Clinard, Marshall B., ed. *Anomie and Deviant Behavior: A Discussion and Critique*. New York: Free Press, 1964.
Clinard, Marshall B., and Peter C. Yeager. *Corporate Crime*. New York: Free Press, 1980.
Clinard, Marshall B., Peter C. Yeager, Jeanne Brissette, David Petrashek, and Elizabeth Harries. *Illegal Corporate Behavior*. Washington, D.C.: Department of Justice, Law Enforcement Assistance Administration, National Institute of Law Enforcement and Criminal Justice, 1979.
Cloward, Richard A. "Illegitimate Means, Anomie, and Deviant Behavior." *American Sociological Review* 24 (1959): 164–176.
Cloward, Richard A., and Lloyd E. Ohlin. *Delinquency and Opportunity: A Theory of Delinquent Gangs*. New York: Free Press, 1960.
Coffee, John C., Jr. "Beyond the Shut-Eyed Sentry: Toward a Theoretical View of Corporate Misconduct and Effective Legal Response." *Virginia Law Review* 63 (1977): 1099–1278.
———. "'No Soul to Damn, No Body to Kick': An Unscandalized Inquiry into the Problem of Corporate Punishment." *Michigan Law Review* 79 (1981): 386–459.
Cohen, Albert K. "The Concept of Criminal Organization." *British Journal of Criminology* 17 (1977): 97–111.
———. *Deviance and Control*. Englewood Cliffs: Prentice-Hall, 1966.
Coleman, James S. *Power and the Structure of Society*. Philadelphia: University of Pennsylvania Press, 1974.
Collins, Randall. "On the Microfoundations of Macrosociology." *American Journal of Sociology* 86 (1981): 984–1014.
Conklin, John E. *Illegal but Not Criminal: Business Crime in America*. Englewood Cliffs: Prentice-Hall, 1977.
Cook, Karen S. "Exchange and Power in Networks of Interorganizational Relations." *Sociological Quarterly* 18 (1977): 1–18.
Corwin, Ronald G. "Organizations as Loosely Coupled Systems: Evolution of a Perspective." Paper presented for Seminar on Educational Organizations as Loosely Coupled Systems, Palo Alto, California, 13–14 November 1976.
Coser, Lewis A., ed. *The Idea of Social Structure: Papers in Honor of Robert K. Merton*. New York: Harcourt Brace Jovanovich, 1975.
Cressey, Donald R. *Other People's Money: A Study in the Social Psychology of Embezzlement*. Glencoe: Free Press, 1953.

Selected Reading

————. "Restraint of Trade, Recidivism, and Delinquent Neighborhoods." In *Delinquency, Crime, and Society,* edited by James F. Short, pp. 209–238. Chicago: University of Chicago Press, 1976.

Demott, D. A. "Reweaving the Corporate Veil: Management Structure and the Control of Corporate Information." *Law and Contemporary Problems* 41 (1977): 182–221.

Denzin, Norman K. "Notes on the Criminogenic Hypothesis: A Case Study of the American Liquor Industry." *American Sociological Review* 42 (1977): 905–920.

Dershowitz, Alan M. "Increasing Community Control over Corporate Crime: A Problem in the Law of Sanctions." *Yale Law Journal* 71 (1961): 289–306.

Dill, William R. "Environment as an Influence on Managerial Autonomy." *Administrative Science Quarterly* 2 (1958): 409–443.

Diver, Colin. "A Theory of Regulatory Enforcement." *Public Policy* 28 (1980): 257–299.

Downey, H. Kirk, and R. Duane Ireland. "Quantitative versus Qualitative: Environmental Assessment in Organizational Studies." *Administrative Science Quarterly* 24 (1979): 630–637.

Duncan, Robert. "Characteristics of Organizational Environments and Perceived Environmental Uncertainty." *Administrative Science Quarterly* 17 (1972): 313–327.

Dynes, R. R., and E. L. Quarantelli. "Organizations as Victims in Mass Civil Disturbances." In *Victimology: A New Focus,* vol. 5, edited by Israel Drapkin and Emilio Viano, pp. 67–77. Lexington, Massachusetts: D. C. Heath, 1974.

Edelhertz, Herbert. *The Nature, Impact, and Prosecution of White Collar Crime.* Washington, D.C.: Department of Justice, Law Enforcement Assistance Administration, National Institute of Law Enforcement and Criminal Justice, 1970.

————. "Transnational White-Collar Crime: A Developing Challenge and Need for Response." *Temple Law Quarterly* 53 (1980): 1114–1126.

Emery, F. E., and E. L. Trist. "The Causal Texture of Organizational Environments." *Human Relations* 18 (1965): 21–32.

Ermann, M. David, and Richard J. Lundman. *Corporate and Governmental Deviance: Problems of Organizational Behavior in Contemporary Society.* New York: Oxford University Press, 1978. 2d ed., rev. 1982.

————. "Deviant Acts by Complex Organizations: Deviance and Social Control at the Organizational Level of Analysis." *Sociological Quarterly* 19 (1978): 55–65.

————. *Organizational Deviance.* New York: Holt, Rinehart and Winston, 1982.

Evan, William M. *Interorganizational Relations.* Philadelphia: University of Pennsylvania Press, 1978.

————. "The Organization-Set: Toward a Theory of Interorganizational Relations." In *Approaches to Organizational Design,* edited by

James D. Thompson, pp. 173–191. Pittsburgh: University of Pittsburgh Press, 1966.

———. *Organization Theory*. New York: Wiley, 1976.

Ewick, Patricia M. "Patterns of Regulatory Enforcement: SEC Sanctioning of Broker-Dealers." Ph.D. dissertation, Yale University, 1983.

———. *Theories of Organizational Illegality: A Reconceptualization*. Yale Working Paper series, vol. 2. New Haven: Department of Sociology, 1981.

Farberman, H. "A Criminogenic Market Structure: The Automobile Industry." *Sociological Quarterly* 16 (1975): 438–457.

Forrest, Thomas R. "Emergent Organization: A New Approach For Study." M.A. thesis, Ohio State University, 1968.

———. *Structural Differentiation in Emergent Groups*. Columbus: Disaster Research Center, Ohio State University, 1974.

Geis, Gilbert. "Deterring Corporate Crime." In *Corporate Power in America*, edited by Ralph Nader and Mark J. Green, pp. 246–258. New York: Viking Press, 1973.

———. "The Heavy Electrical Equipment Antitrust Cases of 1961." In *Criminal Behavior Systems*, edited by Marshall B. Clinard and Richard Quinney, pp. 139–151. New York: Holt, Rinehart and Winston, 1967.

Geis, Gilbert, and Robert F. Meier, eds. *White-Collar Crime: Offenses in Business, Politics, and the Professions*. New York: Free Press, 1977.

Geis, Gilbert, and Ezra Stotland, eds. *White-Collar Crime: Theory and Research*. Sage Criminal Justice System Annuals, vol. 13. Beverly Hills: Sage Publications, 1980.

Gerhart, Peter M. *Report on the Empirical Case Studies Project to the National Commission for the Review of Antitrust Laws and Procedures*. Vol. 2. Washington, D.C.: United States Government Printing Office, 1979.

Gibbs, Jack P. *Norms, Deviance, and Social Control*. New York and Oxford: Elsevier, 1981.

Gouldner, Alvin. "Reciprocity and Autonomy in Functional Theory." In *Symposium on Sociological Theory,* edited by Llewellyn Gross, pp. 241–270. New York: Harper and Row, 1960.

Gross, Edward. "Organizational Crime: A Theoretical Perspective." In *Studies in Symbolic Interaction,* edited by Norman K. Denzin, pp. 55–85. Greenwich, Connecticut: JAI Press, 1978.

———. "Organization Structure and Organizational Crime." In *White-Collar Crime: Theory and Research,* edited by Gilbert Geis and Ezra Stotland, pp. 52–76. Sage Criminal Justice System Annuals, vol. 13. Beverly Hills: Sage Publications, 1980.

Hagan, John, Ilene H. (Bernstein) Nagel, and Celesta Albonetti. "The Differential Sentencing of White-Collar Offenders in Ten Federal District Courts." *American Sociological Review* 45 (1980): 802–820.

162

Harvard Law Review. "Developments in the Law—Corporate Crime: Regulating Corporate Behavior through Criminal Sanctions." *Harvard Law Review* 92 (1979): 1227–1375.

Hay, George A., and Daniel Kelley. "An Empirical Survey of Price Fixing Conspiracies." *Journal of Law and Economics* 17 (1974): 13–39.

Hirschman, A. O. *Exit, Voice, and Loyalty.* Cambridge: Harvard University Press, 1970.

Hollinger, Richard C., and John P. Clark. "The Quality of Work Experience: Its Relationship to Employee Theft and Production Deviance." Paper presented at Society for the Study of Social Problems Annual Meeting, Boston, Massachusetts, 24–27 August 1979.

Katz, Jack. "Cover-Up and Collective Integrity: On the Natural Antagonisms of Authority Internal and External to Organizations." *Social Problems* 25 (1979): 3–17.

———. "Legality and Equality: Plea Bargaining in the Prosecution of White-Collar and Common Crimes." *Law and Society Review* 13 (1979): 431–459.

Kaufman, Herbert. *Red Tape: Its Origins, Uses, and Abuses.* Washington, D.C.: The Brookings Institute, 1977.

King, Deborah Karyn. "Resource Interdependence and Controlling Organizational Deviance: The OCR, Discrimination, and the University." Ph.D. dissertation, Yale University, 1982.

Kramer, Ronald C. "Corporate Crime: An Organizational Perspective." In *White-Collar and Economic Crime,* edited by Peter Wickman and Timothy Dailey, pp. 75–94. Lexington, Masachusetts: Lexington Books, 1982.

Kriesberg, Louis. "Note: Decision-Making Models and the Control of Corporate Crime." *Yale Law Journal* 85 (1976): 1091–1129.

Lange, Andrea G., and Robert A. Bowers. "Fraud and Abuse in Government Benefit Programs." Washington, D.C.: Department of Justice, Law Enforcement Assistance Administration, National Institute of Law Enforcement and Criminal Justice, 1979.

Lawrence, Paul, and Jay Lorsch. *Organization and Environment.* Boston: Harvard University Press, 1967.

Lemert, Edwin M. "Social Structure, Social Control, and Deviation." In *Anomie and Deviant Behavior: A Discussion and Critique,* edited by Marshall B. Clinard, pp. 57–97. New York: Free Press, 1964.

Leonard, William N., and Marvin Weber. "Automakers and Dealers: A Study of Criminogenic Market Forces." *Law and Society Review* 4 (1970): 407–424.

Levine, Sol, and Paul E. White. "Exchange and Interorganizational Relationships." *Administrative Science Quarterly* 10 (1961): 583–601.

Litwak, Eugene, and Lydia Hylton. "Interorganizational Analysis: An Hypothesis on Coordinating Agencies." *Administrative Science Quarterly* 10 (1962): 395–420.

Long, Susan B. "The Internal Revenue Service: Measuring Tax Offenses and Enforcement Response." Washington, D.C.: Bureau of Social Science Research, 1980.

Mann, Kenneth. "Defending White-Collar Crime." Ph.D. dissertation, Yale University, 1980.

Manning, Peter K. "Metaphors of the Field: Varieties of Organizational Discourse." *Administrative Science Quarterly* 24 (1979): 660–671.

———. "Organizational Work: Structuration of Environments." *British Journal of Sociology* 33 (1982): 118–134.

Margolis, Diane Rothbard. *The Managers: Corporate Life in America.* New York: Morrow, 1979.

Marx, Gary T. "Ironies of Social Control: Authorities as Contributors to Deviance through Escalation, Nonenforcement, and Covert Facilitation." *Social Problems* 28 (1981): 222–246.

Meier, Robert F. "Corporate Crime as Organizational Behavior." Paper presented at American Society of Criminology Annual Meeting, Toronto, Ontario, Canada, October 30–November 2, 1975.

Merton, Robert K. "Anomie, Anomia, and Social Interaction: Contexts of Deviant Behavior." In *Anomie and Deviant Behavior: A Discussion and Critique,* edited by Marshall B. Clinard, pp. 213–242. New York: Free Press, 1964.

———. *Social Theory and Social Structure.* Glencoe: Free Press, 1968.

———. "Structural Analysis in Sociology." In *Approaches to the Study of Social Structure,* edited by Peter M. Blau, pp. 21–52. New York: Free Press, 1975.

Metcalf, J. L. "Organizational Strategies and Interorganizational Networks." *Human Relations* 29 (1976): 327–343.

Meyer, Marshall, and Associates. *Environments and Organizations.* San Francisco: Jossey-Bass, 1978.

Moch, Michael, and Stanley E. Seashore. "How Norms Affect Behaviors In and Of Corporations." In *Handbook of Organizational Design,* vol. 1, edited by Paul C. Nystrom and William H. Starbuck, pp. 210–237. New York: Oxford University Press, 1981.

Needleman, Martin L., and Carolyn Needleman. "Organizational Crime: Two Models of Criminogenesis." *Sociological Quarterly* 20 (1979): 517–528.

Olson, Mancur. *The Logic of Collective Action: Public Goods and the Theory of Groups.* Cambridge: Harvard University Press, 1975.

Perez, Jacob. "Corporate Criminality: A Study of the One-Thousand Largest Industrial Corporations in the U.S.A." Ph.D. dissertation, University of Pennsylvania, 1978.

Perrow, Charles. "The Analysis of Goals in Complex Organizations." *American Sociological Review* 26 (1961): 859–866.

Pettigrew, Andrew M. "On Studying Organizational Cultures." *Administrative Science Quarterly* 24 (1979): 570–581.

Pfeffer, Jeffrey. "Administrative Regulation and Licensing: Social Problem or Solution?" *Social Problems* 21 (1974): 468–79.

Selected Reading

Pfeffer, Jeffrey, and Gerald R. Salancik. *The External Control of Organizations: A Resource Dependence Perspective.* New York: Harper and Row, 1978.

Posner, Richard A. "A Statistical Study of Antitrust Enforcement." *Journal of Law and Economics* 13 (1970): 365–419.

Quarantelli, E. L., and Russell R. Dynes. "Organizations as Victims in Mass Civil Disturbances." In *Victimology,* edited by Israel Drapkin and Emilio Viano, pp. 67–77. Lexington, Massachusetts: Lexington Books, 1974.

Quinney, Earl Richard. "Occupational Structure and Criminal Behavior: Prescription Violation by Retail Pharmacists." *Social Problems* 11 (1963): 179–185.

Reisman, Michael W. *Folded Lies: Bribery and Corruption in Multinational Corporations.* New York: Free Press, 1980.

Reiss, Albert J., Jr. "The Study of Deviant Behavior: Where the Action Is." *Ohio Valley Sociologist* 32 (1966): 60–66.

————. "Towards a Revitalization of Theory and Research on Victimization by Crime." *Journal of Criminal Law and Criminology* 72 (1981): 704–713.

Reiss, Albert J., Jr., and Albert D. Biderman. "Data Sources on White-Collar Law Breaking." Washington, D.C.: Department of Justice, National Institute of Justice, 1980.

Reiss, Albert J., Jr., and David J. Bordua. "Environment and Organization: A Perspective on the Police." In *The Police: Six Sociological Essays,* edited by David J. Bordua, pp. 25–55. New York: Wiley, 1967.

Rosenau, James N. "Toward the Study of National-International Linkages." In *Linkage Politics: Essays on the Consequences of National and International Systems,* edited by James N. Rosenau, pp. 44–63. New York: Free Press, 1969.

Ross, G. Alexander. "The Emergence and Change of Organization Sets: An Interorganizational Analysis of Ecumenical Disaster Recovery Organizations." Ph.D. dissertation, Ohio State University, 1976.

Salancik, Gerald R. "The Role of Interdependencies in Organizational Responsiveness to Demands from the Environment: The Case of Women versus Power." University of Illinois, 1976. Mimeographed.

Schelling, Thomas C. "Economic Analysis and Organized Crime." In *Task Force Report: Organized Crime, Annotations, and Consultant's Papers,* pp. 114–126. Washington, D.C.: President's Commission on Law Enforcement and Administration of Justice (1967).

Scherer, F. M. *Industrial Market Structure and Economic Performance,* 2d ed. Chicago: Rand McNally, 1980.

Schrager, Laura Shill, and James F. Short, Jr. "Toward a Sociology of Organizational Crime." *Social Problems* 25 (1978): 405–419.

Selznik, Phillip. *The Organizational Weapon.* Glencoe: Free Press, 1960.

————. *TVA and the Grass Roots.* Berkeley: University of California Press, 1949.

165

Shapiro, Susan S. "Detecting Illegalities: A Perspective on the Control of Securities Violations." Ph.D. dissertation, Yale University, 1980.

———. "Thinking about White-Collar Crime: Matters of Conceptualization and Research." Washington, D.C.: Department of Justice, National Institute of Justice, 1980.

Sherman, Lawrence W. *Scandal and Reform: Controlling Police Corruption.* Berkeley: University of California Press, 1978.

———. "A Theoretical Strategy for Organizational Deviance." Paper presented at Conference on White-Collar and Economic Crime, International Sociological Association, Potsdam, New York, 7–9 February 1980.

———. "Three Models of Organizational Corruption in Agencies of Social Control." *Social Problems* 27 (1980): 478–491.

Shover, Neal. "The Criminalization of Corporate Behavior: Federal Surface Coal Mining." In *White-Collar Crime: Theory and Research,* edited by Gilbert Geis and Ezra Stotland, pp. 98–125. Sage Criminal Justice System Annuals, vol. 13. Beverly Hills: Sage Publications, 1980.

———. "Defining Organizational Crime." In *Corporate and Governmental Deviance: Problems of Organizational Behavior in Contemporary Society,* edited by M. David Ermann and Richard J. Lundman, pp. 37–40. New York: Oxford University Press, 1978.

Simmel, George. *Conflict and the Web of Group Affiliations.* Translated by Kurt H. Wolff and Reinhard Bendix. New York: Free Press, 1956.

Smigel, E. O., and H. R. Ross. *Crime Against Bureaucracy.* New York: Van Nostrand Reinhold, 1970.

Spence, Michael. *Market Signaling.* Cambridge: Harvard University Press, 1974.

Staw, Barry M., and Eugene Szwajkowski. "The Scarcity Munificence Component of Organizational Environments and the Commission of Illegal Acts." *Administrative Science Quarterly* 20 (1975): 345–354.

Stern, Robert N. "Competitive Influences on the Interorganizational Regulation of College Athletics." *Administrative Science Quarterly* 26 (1981): 15–32.

———. "The Development of an Interorganizational Control Network: The Case of Intercollegiate Athletics." *Administrative Science Quarterly* 24 (1979): 242–266.

Stigler, G. J. "The Theory of Economic Regulation." *Bell Journal of Economics and Management Science* 2 (1971): 3–21.

Stinchcombe, Arthur L. "Merton's Theory of Social Structure." In *The Idea of Social Structure: Papers in Honor of Robert K. Merton,* edited by Lewis A. Coser, pp. 11–34. New York: Harcourt Brace Jovanovich, 1975.

———. "Social Structure and Organizations." In *Handbook of Organizations,* edited by James G. March, pp. 142–193. Chicago: Rand McNally, 1965.

Selected Reading

Stone, Christopher D. "Controlling Corporate Misconduct." *The Public Interest* 48 (1977): 55–71.
———. *Where the Law Ends: The Social Control of Corporate Behavior.* New York: Harper and Row, 1975.
Sutherland, Edwin H. "White-Collar Criminality." *American Sociological Review* 5 (1940): 1–12.
———. *White-Collar Crime.* New York: Dryden Press, 1949.
Sykes, Gresham, and David Matza. "Techniques of Neutralization: A Theory of Delinquency." *American Sociological Review* 22 (1957): 664–670.
Terreberry, Shirley. "The Evolution of Organizational Environments." *Administrative Science Quarterly* 12 (1968): 590–613.
Thompson, James D., and William McEwen. "Organizational Goals and the Environment: Goal-setting as an Interaction Process." *American Sociological Review* 23 (1958): 23–31.
Tullock, Gordon. *The Politics of Bureaucracy.* Washington, D.C.: Public Affairs Press, 1964.
Turk, Austin T. "Organizational Deviance and Political Policing." *Criminology* 19 (1981): 231–250.
Turk, Herman. "Interorganizational Networks and Urban Society." *American Sociological Review* 35 (1970): 1–19.
Van Maanen, John. "The Fact of Fiction in Organizational Ethnography." *Administrative Science Quarterly* 24 (1979): 539–550.
Van Maanen, John, and Edgar H. Schein. "Toward a Theory of Organizational Socialization." In *Research in Organizational Behavior,* vol. 1, edited by Barry Staw and L. L. Cummings, pp. 209–264. Greenwich, Connecticut: JAI Press, 1979.
Vaughan, Diane. "Crime between Organizations: A Case Study of Medicaid Provider Fraud." Ph.D. dissertation, Ohio State University, 1979.
———. "Crime between Organizations: Implications for Victimology." In *White-Collar Crime: Theory and Research,* edited by Gilbert Geis and Ezra Stotland, pp. 77–97. Sage Criminal Justice System Annuals, vol. 13. Beverly Hills: Sage Publications, 1980.
———. "Recent Developments in White-Collar Crime Theory and Research." In *The Mad, the Bad, and the Different: Essays in Honor of Simon Dinitz,* edited by Israel L. Barak-Glantz and C. Ronald Huff, pp. 135–147. Lexington, Massachusetts: Lexington Books, 1981.
———. "Toward Understanding Unlawful Organizational Behavior." *Michigan Law Review* 80 (1982): 1377–1402.
———. "Transaction Systems and Unlawful Organizational Behavior." *Social Problems* 29 (1982): 373–379.
Vaughan, Diane, and Giovanna Carlo. "The Appliance Repairman: A Study of Victim-Responsiveness and Fraud." *Journal of Research in Crime and Delinquency* 12 (1975): 153–161.
Warren, Roland. "The Interorganizational Field as a Focus of Investigation." *Administrative Science Quarterly* 12 (1967): 396–419.

Watkins, John C., Jr. "White-Collar Crime, Legal Sanctions, and Social Control: 'Idols of the Theater' in Operation." *Crime and Delinquency* 23 (1977): 290–303.

Weick, Karl E. "Educational Organizations as Loosely Coupled Systems." *Administrative Science Quarterly* 21 (1976): 1–19.

Wheeler, Stanton. "Trends and Problems in the Sociological Study of Crime." *Social Problems* 23 (1976): 525–534.

Wheeler, Stanton, and Mitchell L. Rothman. "The Organization as Weapon in White-Collar Crime." *Michigan Law Review* 80 (1982): 1403–1427.

Whyte, William F. *Street Corner Society.* Chicago: University of Chicago Press, 1955. 3d ed., rev. 1981.

Wickman, Peter, and Timothy Dailey, eds. *White-Collar and Economic Crime.* Lexington, Massachusetts: Lexington Books, 1982.

Wiley, M. G., and M. N. Zald. "The Growth and Transformation of Educational Accrediting Agencies: An Exploratory Study of the Social Control of Institutions." *Sociology of Education* 41 (1968): 36–56.

Williamson, Oliver E. *Corporate Control and Business Behavior: An Inquiry into the Effects of Organization Form on Enterprise Behavior.* Englewood Cliffs: Prentice-Hall, 1970.

————. *Markets and Hierarchies.* New York: Free Press, 1975.

Wilson, James Q., ed. *The Politics of Regulation.* New York: Basic Books, 1980.

Wright, Joseph E. "Interorganizational Systems and Networks in Mass Casualty Situations." Ph.D. dissertation, Ohio State University, 1976.

Yeager, Peter C., and Marshall B. Clinard. "Regulating Corporate Behavior: A Case Study." In *Structure, Law, and Power: Essays in the Sociology of Law,* edited by Paul Brantingham and Jack Kress, chapter 4. Beverly Hills: Sage Publications, 1979.

Yuchtman, Ephraim, and Stanley E. Seashore. "A System Resource Approach to Organizational Effectiveness." *American Sociological Review* 32 (1967): 891–903.

Zald, Mayer N. "On the Social Control of Industries." *Social Forces* 57 (1978): 79–102.

Index

Affirmative action, 102–3
Albonetti, Celesta, 99
Anomie, 55, 60, 61
Authority: internal versus external, 91–92; leakage, 74–75
Autonomy, 88–104, 110; as critical factor in monitoring and investigating, 88; increases probability of organizational misconduct, 107; as masking behavior from outsiders, 89; and mitigation of social control, 103

Becker, Howard, 132
Bill of information, 45–47
Bowers, Robert, 79–80
Bribery, 62
Bureaucracy, problems of, xii

Cloward, Richard, 86
Collective definitional process, 82
Collegial exchange, 133–34
Comparative method, 133, 135
Competition: among Economic Crime Units, 42; as fundamental to economic success, 57–58; as isomorphic process, 35–36; as motivated by social structure, 55; as motivating organizational misconduct, 58–59, 62, 64, 73; for resources, 58, 110; unlimited, 60
Competitive interdependence, 94–101; of agencies and businesses, 100–101; definition of, 103–4; results in compliance, 95; results in increased interdependence, 95

Compliance, 100, 102–3, 104
Computer(s): billing system for welfare on, 10; ease of accounting crimes on, 77–78, 93; and fraud, xii, 1–2, 4, 9; and preedit system required by welfare, 17; use of, for complex transactions, 76
Conflict, organizational, 30–31, 100–101, 120; of interests in Revco case, 48; paradigm, 35–36; between peripheral and primary network organizations, 34
Control. *See* Social Control; Sporadic Control
Cooperation, 100; antagonistic, 31; limitations of, in focused networks, 37; in network organizations, 30–31, 35
Cooptation, 40–42, 46; definition of, 40
Criminogenic transaction system, 81, 84
Culture, organizational, 126–27
Cultural structure, 55
Cultural value, emphasis on success as, 62

Decentralization, 28, 31
Decision making: authority for, 26, 28; constraints on, 42, 57; diffusion of responsibility for, 75; with incomplete information, 78
Deterrence, 110
Deviance, xiii, 23; and social class, 86–87; as motivated by social structure, 55–56; of the privileged, 128
Dexter, L. A., 119
Diversification, 67, 73–74

169